What Growing Up Is All About

A Parent's Guide to Child and Adolescent Development

Ann Vernon
Radhi H. Al-Mabuk

Research Press
2612 North Mattis Avenue
Champaign, Illinois 61821

Cover design by Loren Kirkwood
Composition by Tradewinds Imaging
Printed by McNaughton & Gunn, Inc.

ISBN 0 – 87822–354 –1
Library of Congress Catalog Number 95 – 68368

Contents

Preface

Have you ever wished that your children had come with a set of instructions? Do you sometimes wonder if you are doing the "right" thing as a parent? Do you occasionally feel worried and inadequate about your parenting performance? If you answered these questions in the affirmative, you are not alone! Most parents are concerned about their parenting, and rightfully so. As important as parenting is, most of us have received very little instruction on how to do it. And, since we are dealing with human beings instead of objects, parenting is not as simple as installing a ceiling fan or learning to bake bread.

Parenting is a responsibility people enter into with varying degrees of confidence and competence. And, although it is a serious undertaking, parents do have to be realistic, recognizing that there is no such thing as a perfect parent. In addition, even though parents may do a lot of the right things, children don't always respond as might be expected. Temperament, intelligence, emotional maturity, and developmental abilities influence children's responses to their parents' efforts.

If parents were polled, most would probably say the rewards of parenting far outweigh the frustrations, concerns, disappointments, and confusion. But at the same time, it is very common to hear parents say, "If only I could have done it differently. I wish I hadn't had to learn it all through trial and error."

To be an effective parent, we believe parents must first understand normal child and adolescent development. This information is essential in providing a framework for what to expect from children at various stages. It can have a significant impact on parents' emotional responses to the problems their children present at different stages. By understanding more about developmental stages, parents have a "road map" to refer to in determining whether children or adolescents are reaching their destinations or if they have detoured and need extra support and intervention.

This book aims to offer such guidance. Following a brief introduction, the first chapter in this book discusses general concepts—myths about parenting children and adolescents, emotions and beliefs that interfere with effective parenting, and styles and stages of parenting. The second chapter presents information about communication and discipline. The next four chapters describe characteristics of children and adolescents during specific stages of development: preschool (ages 2 through 5); middle childhood (ages 6 through 11); young adolescence (ages 11 through 14); and mid-adolescence (ages 15 through 18). Examples of typical issues and problems are accompanied by specific, practical suggestions for addressing these concerns. The final chapter concludes with information about several problems that are not necessarily uncommon but fall outside the realm of what most children and adolescents typically experience in the normal growing-up process: Attention Deficit Hyperactivity Disorder (ADHD), suicide, depression, delinquent behavior, eating disorders, drug and alcohol abuse, sexual abuse, and cult involvement.

This book is intended for school and mental health counselors, social workers, and school psychologists to use as a resource with parents in individual consultation or in parent group sessions. In addition, it can serve as a guide for parents who, on their own, want to learn more about what to expect as their children grow up. By reading this book, practitioners and parents can learn more about developmental stages and how to effectively address typical problems of childhood and adolescence.

Introduction

"We're so confused we don't know where to turn," explained frustrated parents to a mental health counselor. "No matter what we do, our eighth grader resists us. Up until last year she was the sweetest child . . . but now she acts like a monster. Her temper tantrums are worse than they were when she was 2, and the foul language she uses is absolutely horrendous. Will she be like this all through high school? What can we do to survive?"

"Why is it," a father asked the school psychologist, "that my 10-year-old son throws a big fit about going to school? He gets good grades and seems to have friends. The only thing he tells me is that he never gets picked to be on a team. Is that such a big deal? Do other kids his age do this, too?"

"I always prided myself on the fact that my daughter seemed so normal. Up until this last year, she was cooperative, responsible, and did well in school. But now that she's in high school, it's all changed. She keeps telling me that she's old enough to make her own decisions and that I don't have a right to know who she spends time with or where she's going. And, to make matters worse, it seems like she goes out of her way to be difficult. If I suggest something, she does the exact opposite. Why is she like this?"

As a parent, you may identify with these scenarios. You may wonder why your child or adolescent acts as he or she does, if

1

the behavior is normal, and what you can do about it. If you discuss your concerns with helping professionals or other parents, you probably breathe a sigh of relief if they reassure you that your son or daughter is acting normally for his or her age, but that may not take away the frustration you experience in not knowing what to do about the situation. Furthermore, you may often feel discouraged because just after you have successfully helped your youngster through one set of issues, another set may arise. If you have several children, you may be on an emotional roller coaster for a long time! Needless to say, your relationship with your children affects all other aspects of your life.

So you won't feel too discouraged, remember that even though family life isn't as simple as it was in the *Leave It to Beaver* days, parents now have more sources of support and more resources. If you are reading this book, you are a well-meaning parent who, like many others, is striving to do your best at a most important job. As you progress through this book, you will learn how to determine whether your child or adolescent's moods, emotions, behaviors, and attitudes are in line with what to expect at different developmental stages. You can also respond to checklists that will give you insight into where your son or daughter fits with others in his or her age range. Sample responses you can make when confronted with typical problems at various stages— for instance, your adolescent's egocentric behavior or your young child's nighttime fears—are included, as are helpful hints for keeping your own sanity while you are trying to save your child's! As for any other life task, parenting has its ups and downs. We hope that by reading this book you will find answers that minimize the downs and maximize the ups.

1

Effective Parenting: Beliefs and Behaviors

"Once upon a time there was a mother and a father who lived in an immaculately clean house with their 10-year-old son and 14-year-old daughter, two cats, and a dog. Every morning over a healthy breakfast, the parents and children chatted about the upcoming day. After Father left for work, Mother took the children to school and returned home to prepare lunch and dinner for the family. When that was done, she did some ironing and cleaning and then picked the children up to take them to their soccer practice and piano lessons. When they returned home, the children did their homework and picked up their rooms without being asked and then sat down to a leisurely dinner with their parents. After dinner they all played board games, and then the children laid out their clothes for school the next day and went to bed without a hassle. Mother and Father discussed their day's events over a cup of coffee before calling it a day."

What's wrong with this picture? Does it fit the contemporary family of the 1990s? Are things leisurely in your household? Do your children do exactly as they should without being told? If you are a mother, do you have the luxury or the desire to stay home? If you are the parent of an adolescent, is your adolescent content to sit around and play board games with you instead of being with friends or talking on the telephone? Is your house immaculately clean? Do you have time to chat about the day's events over the dinner table? Are you even a two-parent family?

We assume that you answered no to several of these questions and instead find your life much different: Your life is hectic, your kids aren't perfect, and neither are you! Frank Main, author of *Perfect Parenting and Other Myths* (1986), emphasizes that the "Mother or Father of the year is a myth, plain and simple, perpetrated by advertisers of detergent, box cakes, floor wax, a variety of TV situation comedies, and of course, by kids" (p. 1).

The dictionary defines *myth* as any imaginary person or thing spoken of as though existing. Let's apply this definition to parents and children, examining the myths that result in frustration and guilt if you don't measure up as the perfect parent or the perfect child.

DISPELLING THE MYTHS

Remember when you were learning to drive a car? Did you expect to know how to do it perfectly the first time? What about when you learned how to swim? Did you just take off, or did you have to learn the strokes and practice them before you mastered the task? For some reason, we expect that we are born with an innate ability to parent—that no one has to teach us how to do it but that we will intuitively know what to do. There isn't anything innate about parenting, except perhaps the feelings of overwhelming awe and joy when you pick up your newborn baby and realize that this is your child. But . . . did you know how to burp the baby correctly, or did someone need to show you? How about putting on a diaper? Was that automatic, or did you need to watch someone do it the first time? What about when that baby cried and wouldn't stop? Did you automatically know why he or she was crying and how to stop it? No, you probably had to experiment a bit, checking to see if the baby was wet or hungry, cold or feverish. And then you tried a variety of interventions. It would have been nice if what you did was guaranteed to work the next time the problem arose, but maybe that wasn't the case and you had to try several different things before you were able to solve that same problem.

In addition to the myth that parenting is innate and we intuitively know what to do, people sometimes mistakenly believe that once you figure out how to parent, it will be smooth sailing from then on. Wrong! Just because you master the diaper changing and the burping routine doesn't mean that the rest will come easily.

With each stage of development new tasks arise for parents as well as children, and the learning starts all over again.

Yet another myth: Even if there is no such thing as a perfect parent, there are perfect kids. Even though on some level parents know this isn't realistic, an amazing number of parents expect perfect grades, clean rooms, stable emotions, punctuality, responsibility (and even enthusiasm) for completing chores, and picture-perfect dress. And that doesn't even begin to tap the list of unrealistic expectations for teenagers—platonic, not sexual, relationships with the opposite sex; no drugs, alcohol, or nicotine; association only with friends who receive the parental stamp of approval; and great achievements after high school. In reality, children may have a lot of these qualities, but when parents hold onto the myth of perfection, they often extrapolate the negatives and blow them out of proportion, failing to see the child or adolescent for what he or she truly is—a fallible human being who has both strong and weak areas.

For those parents who have more than one child, another myth is the effectiveness of "one size fits all" parenting, or the assumption that what works with one child will work with another. Many of you know this just isn't true, in part because all children have different temperaments and personalities and also because, as you become more experienced at parenting, your approaches change. However, many parents still assume that if they used a reward system to motivate one child to do chores that this should work with the next. Maybe and maybe not! It is critical to take into consideration the tremendous individual differences in children, remembering that they each come with a different set of needs and challenges.

Perhaps one of the most difficult myths to dispel is that whatever methods your parents used with you will automatically be best for your child. The problem with this notion is that growing up is a lot more complex today than it was years ago. As children, most of us didn't experience substance abuse as a nearly normal adolescent phenomenon ("Everybody in school drinks"). Nor did we have to worry as much about pregnancy, AIDS, or other sexually transmitted diseases because premarital sex wasn't as common. Decisions about everything were easier to make because there weren't as many choices. Because we live in a more stressful, fast-paced society, life for children and adolescents today is much different. As a result, parenting is more challenging and requires more than an authoritarian "do it now or else" style.

Last but not least is the myth that parenting should be easy. As you read this sentence, you are probably laughing to yourself.

Nevertheless, many parents do think they shouldn't have to work hard at this job. These parents expect that they will employ effective parenting procedures and that their children will automatically respond appropriately. They do not expect failure or setbacks. As unrealistic as this myth is, it is hard to let go of, probably because this is how we wish things would be.

When parents cling to these myths, it is not at all uncommon for them to experience emotional upset such as guilt, anxiety, frustration, anger, or discomfort when things don't happen according to the way they think they should.

IRRATIONAL BELIEFS OF PARENTS

In addition to the myths just described, certain other beliefs have a negative impact on parents' behaviors and emotions. These are called *irrational beliefs*, a concept developed by Albert Ellis. Ellis maintains that to be an effective parent, you must learn to identify and challenge the irrational beliefs that interfere with effective parenting (Ellis, Moseley, & Wolfe, 1966). This process is described in the following paragraphs.

Do you ever think that you are a bad parent if your child misbehaves? Have you ever fallen into the trap of assuming that if your adolescent acts out, he or she is directing the behavior toward you and that it is a personal issue? Have you heard yourself saying, "She should know better . . . how could she do such a dumb thing?" Or have you ever found yourself thinking that if you were a better parent, your child wouldn't have so many problems? Chances are good that you identify with one or more of these statements. If so, you join the ranks of the many parents who get caught in the irrational beliefs trap. While this kind of thinking is not at all uncommon, it is important to learn to challenge it because it almost always results in negative emotions and inappropriate parenting.

You may be asking yourself, "Just exactly what are irrational beliefs?" They are thoughts that result from the following:

1. Demands (things *should* go the way I expect them to; others *must* behave the way I think they should)

2. Self-downing (if something doesn't happen the way it should, it's my fault; I must be perfect)

3. "Awfulizing" or catastrophizing (if something doesn't turn out the way I think it should, it is awful and I can't stand it)

4. Low frustration tolerance or discomfort anxiety (things should come easily to me; I shouldn't have to work too hard at anything, whatever I do shouldn't involve any pain or discomfort)

It is normal to *want* things to go a certain way or to *prefer* that children act the way you want them to, but to *demand* that this be the case is unrealistic because you don't have total control over anyone or anything. Inevitably these demands result in anger. Because anger interferes with effective problem solving, it is better to be able to change your demand ("My son should always do exactly as he is told all of the time") to a preference ("I really hope my son does what I expect of him, but I realize that there are probably times when he won't"). Then, instead of feeling angry, you will feel merely disappointed or irritated. Disappointment and irritation are normal feelings in situations where children don't behave appropriately, and, as a parent, you have a right to do something about the situation. But if you are angry and hang on to your demand that your child should never transgress, you are more likely to behave in an aggressive manner that invites conflict. Letting go of the "should" helps reduce the level of emotional intensity and enables you to deal more effectively with the issue.

Another common trap that parents fall into is the irrational belief that they are to blame for everything that goes wrong. Think about it: Don't you know some fabulous parents who have rotten kids? Or the reverse may be true—wonderful children can have awful parents! The point is that parents do have a tendency to assume total responsibility for the way their children behave, think, and maybe even feel. As a result, when a 14-year-old has a more intense version of the 2-year-old's temper tantrum, parents may put themselves down, thinking that if they were better at parenting their adolescent wouldn't act like this. In reality, this behavior is rather typical for an adolescent and in all likelihood has nothing to do with the parents. However, if the parents take the blame, they may feel guilty, worthless, and incompetent. When this occurs, it is easy for them to give up or to think that nothing they do matters. The problem worsens because if parents are down on themselves, they aren't as effective. The healthy response is to recognize that you are a fallible human being who may try your best but still make mistakes. And, even if you do a perfect job, you aren't in total control of how your offspring choose to think, feel, and behave.

Perhaps the most common irrational belief is the tendency to "awfulize" or catastrophize—in other words, to blow things out of proportion. It is very easy to do this! Have you ever gotten upset when your adolescent was late getting home? All sorts of things might have run through your mind: "He's being defiant," "She was in an accident," "He's being irresponsible," "She's so inconsiderate." The more you thought about it, the more you probably imagined even worse things happening so that by the time your son or daughter walked in the door, your emotions were too stirred up for you to listen to the reasons he or she was late. When you awfulize, you imagine the fantastic worst and don't bother to stop and check out the facts or hypothesize about the various explanations for a given event.

Related to awfulizing is overgeneralizing. When you overgeneralize, you take an isolated event and assume that it will go on forever. For example, you may decide based on one situation that your child will always get bad grades. Or, you might think that your adolescent will never be responsible, based on three incidents within a few months. Whenever you catch yourself overgeneralizing, it is important to stop yourself and ask, "What is the overall pattern? On a routine basis is my child getting bad grades in most subjects? On a routine basis is my adolescent irresponsible?" If you are a visual person, it might help to draw a line on a sheet of paper, labeling one end "always" and the other end "never." Then put a mark on the line to represent where your child's behavior is in relation to these absolutes. This strategy can help you clarify to what extent a problem exists. Observing your child's behavior for a while may show you that you have indeed overgeneralized. And if your observations show that you haven't overgeneralized, you will have some objective information you can use in the problem-solving process.

Even though many parents don't immediately recognize the concept of low frustration tolerance or discomfort anxiety, it is another prevalent irrational belief. Think about how many times you've thought to yourself, "It shouldn't be this hard to parent. I shouldn't have to put up with all these problems." Or you may have thought, "It's just easier to let my child do what she wants than to try to argue with her." Does that ring a bell? It certainly does for a lot of parents who let their children stay up later than they should because it's too much of a hassle to do the bedtime battle or who don't confront their teenagers about their whereabouts because they don't want to experience the discomfort of an obstinate retort. In the long run, this irrational belief results in children's having more power than parents because parents are reluctant to step in and establish boundaries and rules. It becomes very difficult for parents to regain their authority once they realize the situation is out of hand.

Irrational beliefs have a significant impact on how we feel and behave as parents. The following paragraphs outline in more detail specific beliefs that underlie common negative feelings. The information is based on the writings of Michael Bernard (1984) and Jay Barrish and Harriett Barrish (1986).

Anger

Anger, one of the strongest negative emotions parents experience, results in a critical, harsh, authoritarian parenting style. Anger comes from the demand that children must always behave the way we expect them to behave. Notice the overgeneralization here— children must *always* behave as we expect. It is perfectly acceptable to have expectations, but it is unrealistic to demand that children always behave in a certain way, then assume that if they don't it is horrible. This belief also guarantees that as a parent you will spend a lot of time being angry. Do you like being angry? Most parents don't because when they are angry they may say or do things they later regret. In addition, many parents are aware that in the heat of anger their ability to look clearly at options and choose appropriate ones is negatively affected.

Because parents are human beings, they will get angry from time to time. However, it is important to recognize the continuum of emotions, with intense anger at one end, irritation at the other, and varying degrees of emotion in between. In any given situation, examine the circumstances to determine how "horrible" the event really is. For example, is it worth your while to get intensely angry because your child forgets to make his or her bed, or is this something that is just irritating and mildly upsetting? If you believe that your child *should* always do what he or she is told without being reminded, you will probably be very angry. On the other hand, if you expect your child to take care of responsibilities but realize that he or she will forget chores or put them off occasionally, you will feel irritated but not intensely angry. If you express your irritation to your child and work together to help change the behavior, you probably won't have the full-blown battle you would have had if you were very angry and yelled and screamed about how horrible, lazy, and irresponsible your child is.

While some experts believe that getting anger out is important, others propose that doing so only intensifies the anger. They say the more you talk or think about being upset, the angrier you become. Perhaps the most critical factor to weigh is the outcome. In other words, after you have ranted and raged at your child for coming home late or failing a test, how is the relationship between the two of you? If your child is typical, he or she probably raged back at you, and the negative cycle of behavior continued until one of you backed down. Depending on the emotional strength or weakness of the person, the impact of this negative emotional cycle can be long-lasting. Many adults continue to work through the negative feelings they experienced as children when they engaged in frequent battles with their own parents. Some of these battles even may have resulted in physical or verbal abuse. Certainly, all of us would agree that this is not the way to maintain a healthy parent-child relationship.

Can these negative patterns of interaction be avoided? The answer is yes. How? By "talking to yourself," in the process recognizing that while you may not like the behavior, there is no guarantee that your child will always behave the way you expect all the time. By realizing there will be times when your child acts in ways you don't like, you can deescalate your emotion from intense anger to irritation and upset. You can then discuss the incident calmly to request a change in behavior or attitude.

Imagine that your 16-year-old daughter tells you that she is going out with her girlfriend. In reality, you discover that she met her boyfriend and went to a party with him. Note the different outcomes in the two different versions of this scenario:

Version 1

THOUGHTS

She shouldn't lie. She shouldn't try to get by with things she knows we won't approve of. This means we can never trust her again.

FEELING

Anger

Parent: Where were you last night?

Daughter: With Angela at the movie.

Parent: Don't lie to me. I know you were out with your boyfriend. Don't you *ever* lie to me again. You wanted me to trust you? Forget that. Who knows what you did with him. You are grounded for a month, and you cannot speak to that creep you sneaked out with.

Daughter: I hate you. You never let me do anything. You don't understand. I'll never speak to you again.

Version 2

THOUGHTS

I know she is lying, and she will pay the consequences. I don't understand why she just didn't tell us the truth.

FEELINGS

Upset, somewhat angry

Parent: Where were you last night?

Daughter: With Angela at the movie.

Parent: I'd like to believe that, but I know that Angela was home by 11:00 and that you were out with your boyfriend. I am very upset that you lied to me. I am disappointed because I thought I could trust you. You need to know that you will be grounded and that I don't expect you to lie again.

Daughter: I'm sorry I lied. I was just afraid you wouldn't let me see him. I don't think it's fair to ground me.

Parent: I'm sorry you don't think it's fair, but that's the way it is. You shouldn't have assumed that I wouldn't let you see him. I hope we don't have another situation like this.

In the first version, the parent's anger resulted in intense conflict and negativity. In the second, the parent assertively expressed being upset with the situation but avoided hurling accusations and making ultimatums. As a result, the interaction was less hostile. Furthermore, while the parent certainly did not condone lying, there was no *demand* that the daughter *never* lie again. Demands usually don't help the situation.

At times it is difficult not to be angry. However, the more successful you are at changing your *demand* that your child behave in a certain manner to a *preference*, the more you will be able to interact assertively to achieve positive results and maintain a good relationship.

Depression and Guilt

How many times have you felt inadequate as a parent? How often do you hear yourself saying, "If I'd only done this differently, my child wouldn't act that way." Guilt stems from the irrational belief that as a parent, you *should* know exactly what to do all the time and that you *should* be capable of raising a perfect child. The more guilt you feel, the more likely you are to become depressed, thinking that if you are a poor parent you are a worthless person or that when you don't perform adequately as a parent you are a failure. Parents who feel depressed and guilty also assume that their children's problems are all their fault and that if their children misbehave, the misbehavior is directed toward them because their children don't like them.

Guilty parents also incorrectly assume that if they make a mistake it will always negatively affect the child. They may also take total responsibility for their child's problems or think that they could have done something to prevent a disability or problem. At times this could be true, but because parents aren't in total control of how their child thinks, feels, and behaves, they have to understand that they cannot be totally responsible.

As a parent, you must recognize that parenting is only one part of your job and that if you don't do well some of the time as a parent, it does not mean you are a failure as a person. Furthermore, you must understand that when children misbehave (and they will), it does not mean that they will hate you forever. If you are the parent of an adolescent, you must be particularly aware of this because normal adolescents push limits in their struggle for independence. Therefore, keep in mind that your adolescent's behavior is most likely not about you personally.

Parents who feel guilty or depressed may adopt a permissive parenting style, giving in to demands and requests so that their children don't become more upset with them. You will read more about this parenting style later in the chapter.

Discomfort Anxiety

Surely you have known parents who can't stand conflict. As a result, they avoid confronting the child or significant others. For example, we recently talked with a mother who had just discovered that her teenage daughter was sneaking her boyfriend into her room at night. However, since the mother knew that her husband would be furious if he knew about it and that her daughter would throw a fit if she confronted her, this mother chose to ignore the behavior. Her irrational belief was that if something is difficult, it must be avoided. Unfortunately, by enabling her daughter's behavior, she set the stage for a repeat performance.

Certainly none of us enjoys conflict, but we *can* stand it, even if it is uncomfortable. To determine whether you are suffering from discomfort anxiety, take a minute to answer the following questions.

	Yes	No	Sometimes
1. If you ask your child to feed the dog and he doesn't do it after a reminder, do you do it yourself because it's less hassle?	☐	☐	☐
2. If you have set a 12:00 curfew and your daughter comes home at 12:30, do you ignore the time because you don't want to listen to her arguments?	☐	☐	☐
3. If your child is throwing a temper tantrum in the supermarket because he wants a candy bar, do you give in because you don't think you can stand the public embarrassment?	☐	☐	☐
4. If your child forgets her gym clothes and will have to stay after school as a result, do you drop everything and run the clothes to school because you don't want your child to suffer the consequence?	☐	☐	☐
5. If your son is begging you to let him go on the church outing even if he hasn't done all of his chores as he promised, do you give in because you can't stand to see him disappointed or frustrated?	☐	☐	☐

How did you do? If you answered "yes" or "sometimes" to the majority of the questions, you probably are a parent who wants to avoid discomfort. We all want to avoid pain, but avoiding important issues is similar to enabling. It's like hiding our heads in the sand, hoping that the problem will go away. Unfortunately, it seldom does, and it may get bigger.

Parents can have discomfort anxiety not only for themselves but also for their child. In other words, they feel that everything should be easy and free of frustration for the child. Such parents are most likely to be permissive, as you will learn in following discussion of parenting styles.

PARENTING STYLES

Needless to say, not all people parent in the same way. Some adopt the attitudes and behaviors of their parents, while others behave in an opposite manner because they think their parents were overly strict, permissive, unfair, or cruel. Whatever the case may be, your parenting style has been influenced by what your own parents did. Have you ever admonished your child for something or given a "mini-lecture" on the importance of the child's letting you know his or her whereabouts, only to realize that you sound exactly like your mother or father did when you were growing up? Of course, at that time, you were certain that you would never treat your own child this way! And your mother or father may have said, "Just wait until you are a parent. Then you'll know why we get so worried when it's past midnight and we don't know where you are. We assume something bad has happened to you!"

What this implies is that as your role changes, so do your attitudes and behaviors. In addition, since parenting children in the 1990s is in many ways much more challenging than it was when you were a child, you will have to assimilate new information and skills to deal with problems and issues that your parents probably didn't confront. For example, most of your parents didn't have to worry about teenage drinking and premarital sex. They most likely did not even think about drug use as you were growing up, nor was suicidal behavior as much of a concern.

To learn more about parenting styles, and yours in particular, take a few minutes to complete the following questionnaire. Circle the letter that best represents your response to each question.

1. If your son comes home with a bad grade, are you more likely to be:
   (a) harsh *or*
   (b) understanding in your response to this situation?

2. If your daughter doesn't do assigned chores, are you more likely to:
   (a) ground her for not completing the task *or*
   (b) do the chore yourself?

3. When you are trying to carry on a conversation with guests and your 5-year-old keeps interrupting, are you more likely to:
   (a) teach your child when it is appropriate to interrupt *or*
   (b) chastise your child and send him from the room?

4. If your adolescent starts hanging out with friends you find less than desirable, do you:
   (a) listen to the explanation about the selection of friends but express your concerns in a firm, caring way *or*
   (b) forbid your adolescent to associate with these friends and threaten to ground her?

5. If your child talks back to you, are you more likely to:
   (a) take responsibility for why the child is acting this way, thinking that it's because you as a parent aren't loving enough *or*
   (b) send him to his room, threatening grounding if there is more of this kind of behavior?

6. If your child consistently does a sloppy job mowing the lawn, are you more likely to:
   (a) avoid confrontation *or*
   (b) have a direct but gentle talk with her?

Your responses to these types of situations can give you an idea of what kind of parent you generally are. The following styles correspond to the following answers:

1. (a) authoritarian
   (b) authoritative

2. (a) authoritative
   (b) permissive

3. (a) authoritative
   (b) authoritarian

4. (a) authoritative
   (b) authoritarian

5. (a) permissive
   (b) authoritarian

6. (a) permissive
   (b) authoritative

Two dimensions help identify your parenting style: warmth and control. If you exercise a high degree of control and a low level of warmth, you are said to be *authoritarian*. If you display warmth and a reasonable degree of control, your parenting style is known as *authoritative*. Your parenting style is *permissive* if you exhibit low control but a high degree of warmth. And, if you are low on both control and warmth, your parenting style is *ignoring*.

Authoritarian

The authoritarian parent disciplines a child for misbehavior through punishment, which is sometimes very harsh. This type of parent uses anger to try to change behavior. The authoritarian parent believes he or she is always right and that children should never disagree or argue. The children receive very little warmth (few hugs, kisses, or positive expressions of support and caring) and are always kept under a tight grip. An authoritarian parent might say to a child, "You do it my way or else." The authoritarian parent does not invite discussion, behaving instead like a dictator.

The consequences of authoritarian parenting are generally very negative. Although the children of authoritarian parents may be well behaved, the parent-child relationship is very tense and there is very little evidence of mutual caring. Instead, the children of such parents tend to be either inhibited and fearful or rebellious. They may readily succumb to peer pressure, especially when the behavior in question is antisocial. They are more likely to abuse drugs, to have poor self-esteem and communication skills, and to do poorly in school. While they might not express their anger directly, it is constantly beneath the surface, commonly displayed as general unhappiness. Moreover, they are likely to become authoritarian parents themselves.

Authoritative

Authoritative parents display warmth toward their children. They give assurances of worth and value, meanwhile maintaining a reasonable amount of control. Children of authoritative parents are encouraged to be independent and are usually invited to discuss concerns or areas of disagreement with their parents.

Authoritative parents have clear expectations and reasonable rules and consequences, many of which are jointly developed with the child. There is mutual respect. In a discipline situation, an authoritative parent might put an arm around the child in a comforting way and say, "You know you shouldn't have done that. Let's talk about how you can handle the situation better next time."

Children reared by authoritative parents fare the best. They are competent, confident, self-reliant, and socially responsible. They also feel positive about themselves. Because they recognize that their parents will generally treat them reasonably, they are less likely to lie or try to hurt their parents through rebellious, antisocial, or self-destructive behavior.

Permissive

Permissive parents display warmth toward their children but are very low in control. Permissive parents are generally uninvolved in their child's life, believing that it is best not to interfere and create a conflict. The philosophy of the permissive parent can best be summarized as follows: "Conflict is bad and just creates more problems. Therefore, it is easier to just let things go so that everyone can be happy." Unfortunately, it doesn't work quite this way! If parents simply allow their children to do as they please, parents ultimately become upset because the children aren't following minimal rules or responding in a positive way. In addition, children of permissive parents are often very anxious because rules aren't clear or consistent. As a result, they often don't know what to expect. While it may seem as though children would be happiest under this style of parenting, many children, particularly adolescents, act out in varying degrees to reestablish an appropriate parent-child hierarchy of authority. Developmentally, children are not capable of making all of the rules themselves, and, even though they might not act like it at all times, they experience a certain amount of relief from knowing who is in charge and what is expected of them.

When children of permissive parents misbehave, the parents often overlook the misbehavior. If they do confront it, they give in when their children argue with them about the rules or consequences. Children of permissive parents know that even if their parents threaten to ground them, it won't last. They know that if they whine or argue or threaten, their parents will give in. Because permissive parents don't establish rules or follow through with the rules they have, their children often have the mistaken belief that their parents don't really care what they do. This frequently results in socially incompetent behavior, especially a lack of self-control.

Ignoring

Ignoring parents cannot answer the question "It is 10:00 P.M. Do you know where your child is?" These parents are unaware that their children have a strong need for parents to care about them. Children of ignoring parents are often left to their own devices with very little parental guidance. Ignoring parents put their own needs first. Although it certainly isn't bad to put yourself first some of the time, in this case, the message is "Children are a bother, and my life would be a lot better if I didn't have to deal with them."

Children of ignoring parents may go to extremes to get their parents to pay attention to them. They may fail at school, act out, abuse drugs, cheat, steal, or become sexually promiscuous. By provoking their parents' anger, such children at least prove that their parents care enough to get angry. Unfortunately, these behaviors generate a multitude of other problems and create further complications in the parent-child relationship. These children also lack social competence and have low self-esteem.

LONG-RANGE AND SHORT-RANGE PARENTING

Jane Nelsen and Lynn Lott (1991) discuss parenting styles in another way—in terms of the long- and short-term impact for the child. In brief, parenting that is long-range and farsighted results in responsible children with skills that will serve them well in life. Short-range parenting results in children who become codependent, rebellious, unhealthy, and adult pleasers.

The Long-Range Approach

Parents who practice long-range parenting do things with their children, are involved in their lives to a reasonable extent, and are not overcontrolling. Parents and children deal with power in a win-win fashion. Problems that arise are solved collectively, through family meetings and discussions. Long-range parenting uses natural consequences for inappropriate behavior. Understanding the relationship between their behavior and consequences helps children learn what they can do to change situations for the better.

Parents who adhere to this parenting style don't enable their children. In other words, they don't do everything for their children or buffer them from the real world. They don't encourage unhealthy dependence or prevent their children from learning to do things for themselves. Instead, these parents believe that it is important to prepare children for future roles in society by helping them take responsibility for their own behavior and by encouraging and empowering them. According to Nelson and Lott, empowerment invites kids to think for themselves, to learn to make their own decisions, to consider consequences, and to live with their mistakes. Through empowerment, children develop the courage to hang in when things get tough, the responsibility to face mistakes, and the ability to cooperate with others.

Parents with a long-range perspective give their children unconditional love, respect their thoughts and feelings without always agreeing with them, share feelings, and try to listen to their children's perspectives without passing judgment or stifling communication. Even though there are difficult periods, such parents have faith in their children and let them know they are cared about.

The Short-Range Approach

Parents who practice a short-range parenting style are not teaching children the skills they need to become independent adults. By doing things for, or to, their children, parents are trying to "fix" problems instead of helping the youngsters develop skills themselves. For example, a parent with a short-range view might write an excuse for his daughter who skipped school rather than allow her to face the consequences of her own behavior, thereby enabling the behavior. The parent may do this because the daughter might throw a fit if he refuses to write the excuse. On the other hand, such a parent might ground the daughter for a month for skipping school. Because this form of punishment is unrelated to the misbehavior, it also does not teach the adolescent how to be responsible for her actions.

This type of parenting is a blend of both the authoritarian and permissive parenting styles. Controlling through punishments that

are unrelated to the situation is a common short-term parenting practice. When control does not yield the desired results, a parent with
a short-range perspective may just give up in total frustration and,
lapsing into permissiveness, let the child do what he or she wants.

Short-term parenting may also be overprotective. Parents do
things for their children that the children should be responsible
for themselves. Consider this scenario: Your sixth grader habitu-
ally forgets his homework and calls you to bring it to school. Do
you do it? If you do, you are not teaching your child to be
responsible and face the consequences of not having the homework at school. Chances are that this behavior will keep occurring because there is no reason for him to do otherwise. However,
if you express that you are sorry that he was not better organized and agree to help him work out a plan to avoid this problem again, you are teaching an important skill.

Another form in which this parenting style is expressed is
neglect of the child through indifference to the child's physical,
emotional, or mental well being. Other manifestations include
aloofness, emotional unavailability, and lack of communication.
Such reactions often result from ignorance or misguided beliefs
about appropriate ways to respond to children.

In problem-solving situations, parents with a short-range
view tell children what to do and try to solve their problems for
them, thereby robbing children of the chance to rely on themselves. Mistakes are not tolerated; the parents insist that things
be done their way. Children are bossed, nagged, and pressured
to follow the parents' way, and in response they either give in or
rebel. In turn, the parents respond with more stringent rules and
stiffer punishments. Children view their parents as judgmental
and their love as conditional: "My mom or dad will love me as
long as I do things her or his way."

Such parents are also overly concerned about what others
might think of them. They want to look good and be perceived as
good parents. They also want to protect their children from pain
and may think they are being selfish if they aren't self-sacrificing.

STAGES OF PARENTING

Tied closely to the concept of parenting styles is the notion that
there are stages in parenting. Each stage is characterized by particular demands, challenges, and rewards. One's professed parenting style is put to test during these stages.

Both children and parents go through stages. Parental stages begin even before a child is born and continue throughout life. Even when your children are autonomous adults, the process of parenting continues. You never stop being a parent. Furthermore, your beliefs and parenting style evolve as you move through the stages. Ellen Galinsky, author of *Between Generations: The Six Stages of Parenthood* (1981), identifies the following stages of parenting: image making, nurturing, authority, interpretive, interdependent, and departure. As you read on, see if you can identify which stage you are currently experiencing. You may be in two or more stages simultaneously if you have more than one child.

Image-Making Stage

Galinsky maintains that this stage occurs during the pregnancy. As a soon-to-be parent, you begin to formulate ideas of what your life will be like and how your roles will change. In reality, this stage might begin earlier, as you observe parents with children and speculate on what it would be like if you were in their shoes. It could even begin further back in childhood, when you played house and pretended you were a parent. At any rate, the image-making stage is an important one because it is here that you begin to formulate your vision of parenting.

Although the degree to which image making occurs may vary depending on the amount of introspection an individual engages in, most expectant parents do think about what will change after the arrival of the baby. Perhaps the most significant changes concern the impact of parenthood on one's identity as a parent, the relationship with one's spouse, and the relationship with one's own parents. A danger during this stage is speculating too much and becoming anxious about how different things could be. On the other hand, if these issues are not anticipated to some degree, new parents sometimes find it difficult to handle the changes.

Many times, parents-to-be search through their memories of childhood, recalling how they were parented and how they would like to change or maintain this parenting style. Do you remember swearing that you would never raise your child as you were raised, but as time goes on, beginning to sound more and more like your parents? The reason for this, of course, is that as a new parent, you are in the "honeymoon" stage, and as you learn by experience, you sometimes find out that attaining your ideal is not as easy as it once looked!

Parental image making is also influenced by a number of other factors, such as whether the child was planned or not and cultural expectations that shape our ideas about the type of parents we should be.

It is important for parents to have flexible images that can be changed to match reality. Galinsky cautions that some parents may suffer severe depression and even abuse their children if they inflexibly adhere to an image that conflicts with reality. For example, if your image is that children will be well behaved and obedient all of the time, it will be easy to become depressed or turn your anger against the child. In addition, it is important to be able to change behavior in order to come closer to attaining a desired image. For instance, if you had the image of yourself as a supportive, nurturing parent and instead were angry and punitive, you would want to take steps to modify your behavior to fit more with your original image.

Nurturing Stage

The second stage, beginning with the birth of the baby and continuing until the child is about 2 years old, is called the nurturing stage. During this stage, the parents become attached to the baby and reconcile the image of the child they formed during pregnancy with the child that is born. The reconciliation occurs by interacting with the child—by holding, touching, talking to, and caring for the baby. Through these interactions, parents bond with their baby; they form and nurture a relationship with the child. It might take a while for parents to believe that the new baby is really theirs, feel close to the baby, feel confident they can take care of the baby, and generally get to know the baby.

The parent-child relationship is a reciprocal one. What your child does affects what you do, which in turn affects what the child does. It is useful to remember that every child is different—some require more sleep than others, for example. The image of the child that you have formed must be modified to be consistent with the real child's personality.

A word of caution: Do not forget yourself, your partner, your other children (if any), and others in your life as you bond with your new baby. Introducing a new member into a household can be stressful, and the family dynamics will change. By being aware of this and taking time to nurture other relationships and yourself, you will be less likely to overreact to the stress.

Authority Stage

The authority stage corresponds with the child's preschool years—from about age 2 through 5. The primary task during this stage is deciding what constitutes parental authority, how to establish rules, what rules to set, when and how to enforce these rules, and what to do when rules are violated.

Parents now confront the issue of authority and power as they find their child testing the rules they set. To resolve this issue, parents must examine the images they formed during the image-making stage: Did they assume that parents should never get angry? Did they see themselves as always being kind and affirming? Did they see their child as always being helpful and perfect? These images will need to be "reality tested" in order to formulate reasonable rules and expectations and to exercise reasonable parental authority.

During this stage, it is helpful to be deliberate and conscious about how to handle authority because doing so can have an impact on the self-concept of both parent and child. Successful resolution of the authority stage means knowing what rules to set, determining when and how to implement them, and having specific consequences for rule violation.

Interpretive Stage

This fourth stage begins as the child enters school and ends as adolescence approaches. The task at this stage is for parents to evaluate how realistic they have been by reviewing the past and pondering the future. As they engage in self-evaluation about their parental role, they may find it necessary to revise the way they view parenting. This in turn may lead to the formation of new images or expectations for the future. For example, as the child enters school, many parents become concerned about the development of the child's self-concept, social skills, and academic strengths. They become concerned about what values to instill in the child and how much guidance they need to provide. For the first-time parent, this is all new territory, and there are no easy answers. Issues relating to expectations about the child's performance and participation in sports, activities, lessons, or clubs must be examined in light of what is best for the child. While these expectations are usually based on the former images of the child, it may be necessary to reevaluate these.

This stage concludes the childhood years and ushers in a new stage—the teenage years. Many parents look back on the previous years with regret and nostalgia—and ahead with appre-hension and anticipation. During this period parents begin to form new images of themselves as the parents of a teenager and start to rehearse for this role.

Interdependent Stage

The interdependent stage spans the teenage years. Issues that emerged during the authority stage may need to be reevaluated as the teenager pushes limits. In addition, because the adolescent is changing in so many ways, parents find themselves compelled to adjust their image of the child. For example, the once-obedient, loving daughter may now be an obnoxious, mouthy teenager. This change may surprise and even shock many parents because it shatters their existing image of the child. However, it is impor-tant to be flexible and remember that the interdependent stage won't last forever. Overgeneralizing about how horrible things are won't help matters.

At this stage, parents must establish a new type of relation-ship with their son or daughter in order to meet the challenges that characterize this stage of development. A teenager will probably behave disrespectfully at times, test limits, and engage in behav-iors that worry parents. Parents often find themselves dealing with problems that they feel unable to handle.

The demands of this stage require parents to engage in more effective patterns of communication, set appropriate but reason-able limits, and provide guidance while at the same time "letting go." Parents need to understand that the push toward autonomy reflects the teenager's need to establish an identity separate from the parents.

Departure Stage

With the conclusion of the teenage years comes the departure stage, in which images are made about the future—one without the child. This is a crucial stage in that parents assess their suc-cesses and failures in raising the child and determine whether they have adequately prepared the child for the adult years. During this stage, parents begin to anticipate and rehearse for their child's leaving home. After the child leaves, parents must adapt to the departure.

Images that could interfere with effective resolution of this stage include the notions that the leaving home and resettling process will be smooth or that once the child has left, he or she is gone for good. It can also be a problem if parents assume that the child will necessarily become a parent, be successful, and/or take care of them in their old age.

Different parents come out of this stage feeling different things. Some may be confused. Some may feel hurt. Some may be pleased with how they have raised their children thus far. Whatever the outcome, all parents have experienced significant changes during the course of parenting their children through the childhood and adolescent years.

CONCLUSION

As a result of reading this chapter, you have had the opportunity to reflect on yourself as a parent. You have read about many of the myths of parenting and have learned that parents often have irrational beliefs that can interfere with effective parenting. If you were a dedicated reader, you completed some self-assessment questions about your parenting style and learned about the authoritative, authoritarian, permissive, and ignoring parenting styles. You also considered the difference between short-term and long-term parenting approaches.

This first chapter has offered reassurance that while parenting isn't an easy job that comes with clear instructions, certain attitudes, behaviors, and parenting styles can make the job more manageable. The next chapter presents some information on communication and discipline. As you read, remember that you may need to tailor techniques to your individual style, taking into consideration the personality of your child and the dynamics of the situation.

2

Back to the Basics: Communication and Discipline

Parent: *(To child)* Where have you been? I've been looking everywhere for you. Why can't you ever let me know where you're going?

Child: *(To parent)* Gee, Mom! I *told* you I was going to ride my bike to the park. You *never* listen to me.

Parent: *(To child)* Don't talk back to me, young man, or you won't be riding your bike anywhere.

Have you had the "you never listen to me" accusation thrown in your face a few times? Most parents have . . . and they also think their children never listen to them. Likewise, the "don't talk back to me" threat may occasionally have come out of your mouth.

This chapter presents practical suggestions to enhance effective parent-child communication, followed by some discipline "do's" and "don'ts." However, regardless of how adeptly you apply these "user-friendly" communication and discipline strategies, there are no foolproof methods. Patience and practice of these methods will be required before you see the payoffs with your child.

COMMUNICATION TECHNIQUES THAT DON'T WORK

It is impossible to avoid disagreements with children and adolescents, but you can prevent them from destroying your relationship when you communicate effectively. Although this sounds simple, effective communication is more difficult than it seems. Most parents don't intentionally try to block communication; we inadvertently fall into communication traps based on what we may have experienced growing up or on what comes naturally. Thomas Gordon, author of *Parent Effectiveness Training* (1970), identifies the following "typical twelve" communication roadblocks.

Ordering, Directing, Commanding

"Shut off that stupid TV and get your homework done."

"Do it because I said so."

If you were to ask children or adolescents how they feel when they are talked to in this manner, they would unanimously say resentful or angry. Orders and commands put children on the defensive and invite argument. This is not to say that as a parent you don't have the right to ask that something be done. You do. However, a simple "please" and a neutral tone of voice work better than a command.

Warning, Admonishing, Threatening

"If you don't stop that, you won't leave this house."

"You'd better shape up, or you're in for big trouble."

Certainly, parents need to admonish their children periodically, but it is better to phrase your warnings in terms of politely stated consequences: "If you don't stop teasing your sister, you will need to go to your room." Keeping your anger in check so that your tone of voice isn't hostile and threatening is the fine-line distinction between issuing a warning and describing a consequence.

Moralizing, Preaching

"You shouldn't be so rude."

"You should know better than to skip classes. How many times have I told you about this?"

It is hard for parents not to preach, but preaching can have two negative results. First, it can cause shame because the child is reminded of what he or she should or shouldn't have done. Second, children—adolescents in particular—tend to tune out preaching because it interferes with their ability to make judgments they feel they are capable of making. To them, it is demeaning. Rather than preach, it is better for parents to express a concern as an "I" message and a request: "I don't appreciate your rude behavior, and I expect it to stop." ("I" messages will be discussed in more detail later in this chapter.)

Advising, Giving Solutions or Suggestions

"If you'd do your project this way, it would be better."

"Why don't you ask the boy next door over to play?"

It is impossible for parents not to advise, but heavy doses of advice interfere with a young person's ability to learn problem-solving techniques. Given too much advice, children relinquish ownership of the outcome and may blame the advice giver if the situation doesn't turn out right. Rather than give advice, it is preferable to ask children what they think they could do to improve their project or what they had thought about doing with their free time. Granted, giving advice and making suggestions are more expedient, but in the long run they rob children of an important learning opportunity. It is good to remember that independent problem solving increases with age and maturity, so it is more appropriate to give advice to very young children than to older children.

Lecturing, Teaching, Giving Logical Arguments

"When I was your age, I helped my parents all the time."

"If you learn how to be responsible now, it will help you in the future."

Kids resent lectures. They will tell you that they hear enough of them in school. The older they get, the more they resist the logical argument and do their best to find every possible loophole. The bottom line is that this practice doesn't result in good parent-child communication. The rule of thumb is simply to avoid this strategy!

Judging, Criticizing, Disagreeing, Blaming

"That was a stupid thing to do."

"Because you were so late bringing the car
home, you ruined our day."

It appears obvious that these techniques are classic put-
downs that create hostility, shame, resentment, and low self-
worth. The negative effects of judgment, criticism, and blame
can be long-lasting. Certainly there are times when you and your
child will disagree, but when you do, state your disagreement as
a matter of opinion: "I know you don't think there is anything
wrong with wandering the streets late at night, but I am concerned about your safety."

Praising, Agreeing

"Well, even though you think you're dumb,
I know you are smart."

"You can do well if you try."

No amount of praise will make children feel confident and
capable if they themselves have low self-esteem. Even though
you think they can do something if they try, they may not
believe it. They may feel as though they are letting you down
even more if they try and fail. It is better to let children express
their feelings about why they think they cannot succeed and
then help them look for concrete evidence of past successes.
When they do well, express your feelings by saying, "I had confidence in you, and I am proud of what you did."

Name-calling, Ridiculing, Shaming

"You're just acting like a baby."

"You look absolutely ridiculous with your hair
that way."

No one likes to be ridiculed or called names, especially when
it comes from family members children assume love them. The
negative effects of these techniques are very powerful—loss of
self-esteem, resentment, and humiliation.

Interpreting, Analyzing, Diagnosing

"You're just saying that to make me upset."

"You're hanging out with those creeps because
you feel so inferior."

It is best to avoid these techniques because your interpreta-
tion or analysis is based on assumptions that may or may not be
true. Rather than practice these techniques, express your concern
in a straightforward manner and invite a response from your
child about the purpose of his or her behavior.

Reassuring, Sympathizing, Consoling, Supporting

"Don't worry, everything will work out."

"Even if your boyfriend doesn't call today,
I'm sure he'll call tomorrow."

Like praising and agreeing, you may think that these are positive techniques. However, reassurance is sometimes false . . .
things may not work out. It is better to say, "I know you are worried, and I hope things work out. Maybe we can think of some
more solutions."

Sympathy implies a "you poor thing" attitude: "You poor
thing—I know you wanted to win that election." Empathy is better
because you feel *for* the child without feeling sorry for him or her:
"I know that it's painful for you to lose the election."

Consoling and supporting can be appropriate as long as you
don't imply that the child can't deal with the problem at some
point. Sometimes well-meaning parents console and support to
the point where they create dependency.

Probing, Questioning, Interrogating

"Why weren't you home on time?"

"Why didn't you tell your friends you couldn't play?"

Children—adolescents in particular—will tell you that they
sometimes feel they are playing "20 Questions" with their parents—
and they don't like it. Granted, you do have to ask questions, but
try your best to avoid "why" questions because they put children

on the defensive. Young people also share that parents start bombarding them with questions the minute they walk in the door: "How was your day?" "Did you play with your friend?" "What did you have for lunch?" Many children respond with a monosyllable or a few words—"Fine," "No," "I don't remember"—because they resent the questions. Sometimes one question is enough to initiate a conversation, and many parents find that if they don't push the issue, their children will volunteer information at their own pace.

Withdrawing, Distracting, Diverting, Being Humorous

"Oh, let's just forget about it."

"If you let your hair grow any longer, they'll think you're a girl."

Distracting, withdrawing, and diverting are temporary solutions at best, and humor can sometimes be taken the wrong way. If your child is really upset about something and needs to talk it through, withdrawing from the situation or using distraction or humor to change the focus doesn't make the problem go away. These techniques may be appropriate if you sense that the child is on overload and just can't discuss the issue any more, but for the most part it is better to deal with problems than to avoid them.

COMMUNICATION TECHNIQUES THAT DO WORK

Kids complain that parents nag, play the "blame game," and talk excessively. Parents are upset because their children, particularly adolescents, don't open up to them. Kids argue that parents stifle communication when they are sarcastic or say, "See, I told you so." Parents say they feel frustrated when they do try to communicate and their children respond with "Nothing," "I don't want to talk about it," or "Leave me alone." Kids say parents don't give them a chance to explain anything before they start lecturing, jumping to conclusions, or assuming things that aren't true. Parents are confused because they never seem to be doing the right thing. All of these feelings can be the result of ineffective communication.

Communication is a two-way street, and effective communication is essential for healthy relationships. The following paragraphs describe practices that enhance communication.

"I" Messages

Perhaps the most effective key to good communication is to use "I" messages as opposed to "you" messages (Gordon, 1970). "I" messages are nonjudgmental statements about how we feel, whereas "you" messages are accusations or evaluations of someone's behavior, attitudes, or motives. The "you" is easy to deliver and may sound familiar: "You stop that," "You should act your age," "Why can't you just use your head?" or "Don't you ever stop to think about how others feel?" "You" messages invite defensiveness and don't necessarily communicate what you feel. Furthermore, "you" messages don't get you any closer to the goal of open parent-child communication.

What's so great about "I" messages? First, they clearly communicate how you are feeling to your child without putting the child down or on the defensive. Second, they are more effective than shaming and blaming because they give the child the option of changing behavior without losing face. Perhaps most important, "I" messages usually cause less resistance and resentment and offer a better chance of maintaining good feelings and open communication.

Let's look at the difference between these two types of messages by considering the following scenario: Your adolescent daughter promised to call by 9:00 P.M. to let you know where she was and what she was doing so you could discuss what time she should be home. She left the house at 7:00 P.M., but by 11:00 P.M. she still hasn't called. At 11:30 P.M. she finally calls, saying that she is at the bowling alley and asking if she can come home at 12:30 A.M. The following dialogue illustrates a "you" message in response to this situation.

> Parent: What do you think you're doing, calling at 11:30? Can't you think of anyone but yourself? What right do you think you have to call *now* and then expect to stay out later? You get home right now.

> Daughter: I didn't know what we were going to do, and I just forgot. You treat me like a baby anyway. Why should I have to call when none of my friends do? You're being unfair.

> Parent: Talk about unfair. I'm the one who has to sit up and worry about where you are and what you're doing. Don't argue with me. If you're

not home in 15 minutes, you'll be grounded
for a month.

Think about this conversation. Was anything resolved? Is the parent-child relationship good? What kind of atmosphere will exist once the daughter hits the doorstep?

In contrast, let's look at the same scenario with the parent using an "I" message.

> Parent: I'm upset because I asked you to let me know by 9:00 P.M. who you were with and what you planned to do. I felt that I was being reasonable about that because I realized that you were just going to hang out a while and then decide what to do. I feel angry that you waited so long to call and that now you are asking to stay out later.

> Daughter: I'm sorry. We were just listening to music and then sort of walked over here, and I forgot to call.

> Parent: I'm sorry, too, but I've been worried and upset. I will expect you home in 15 minutes. I hope you realize that if you can't follow the rules, I can't allow you to have as much freedom. Please think about that, and we can discuss it more when you get home.

You may be thinking that this doesn't sound like something you could do! Initially, "I" messages may sound a bit forced and awkward, particularly if you're a past master of the "you" message. However, don't dismiss the idea without trying it. When you deliver the "I" message you increase understanding by trying to recognize the adolescent's point of view while at the same time communicating your own thoughts and feelings. Expressing your feelings is important because most children are sensitive to what their parents are feeling, and understanding their parents' feelings helps them comprehend why their parents are behaving as they are. Although the response will depend on the child's personality and the history of the parent-child relationship, the "I" message is less likely to invite hostility.

To deliver a good "I" message, parents have to set aside their tendency to judge, assume, and blame. They must stay clear about how they are feeling and why, and then give the message by using a formula such as the following: "When you _____ *(describe the behavior in a nonjudgmental way)*, I feel _____ *(describe your feelings)*, because _____ *(share what effect the behavior has on you)* "

Following this formula can open the door to better communication and can help you initiate problem solving and request behavior change. Some parents have found it more effective to start by sharing their feelings, then describing the behavior and its effect: "I feel angry and frustrated when you wait until the last minute to do your homework and then want my help at a time that isn't convenient."

Try to be specific when you describe the behavior that upsets you. Rather than say, "When your room is a disaster . . . " say, "When your clothes aren't picked up off the floor and you have left food to rot in the room . . . " If instead of being specific you blow the situation out of proportion, you are more likely to invoke an argumentative response such as "My room is not a total disaster—there are only a few clothes on the floor."

In addition, it is important to stay objective and be brief. Make one point at a time so your child is clear about what you are concerned about. Instead of saying, "I'm upset that you leave your bike in the driveway in the path of the car and that you never feed your pets," it's better to say, "I'm upset that you leave your bike in the driveway in the path of the car," then wait until later to raise another issue. Also, use words that accurately describe your feelings. Are you angry or just annoyed? Are you worried instead of angry? Try to be precise.

One final point about effective messages: Be as concrete as possible in describing the effects of the child's behavior. If your child's behavior cost you money, added extra time or work, or interfered with your plans, let that be known without sounding accusatory. For example, you might say, "I was annoyed when you didn't pick up your room when I asked because it created more work for me. I had to do an extra load of laundry when you finally cleaned."

Active Listening

Besides delivering your message, another key component of good communication is active listening. Kids want parents to listen, and many of them will say that parents talk too much. It is very easy to do this because as parents we want to jump in and reassure, give advice, or ask questions. But in the long run, this turns kids off to the point that many of them, especially adolescents, will go to their friends if they want someone to listen. This is natural to some extent, but most families who seek counseling list open communication as the number one priority for improving relationships.

What is active listening? It is paying attention rather than focusing on other things; showing that you are interested by making eye contact, nodding your head, and smiling if appropriate; and using encouragers, such as "I understand," "Really?" and "Um-hum."

Active listeners recognize that in addition to hearing the words that are spoken they need to watch body language and pay attention to tone of voice. A youngster might tell you that she really isn't upset about not being invited to a birthday party, but as she says that, you may notice that her eyes tear up. Believe what you see and gently point out that you can see the tears and guess that she might, in fact, be more upset than she realizes.

As an active listener, you may have to bite your tongue to resist the temptation to interrupt with questions or comments or to defend your point of view. It is far better to hear the speaker out. When children are upset, they just want someone to listen and understand. Especially in situations where there isn't an easy solution, an understanding response may be all it takes, as illustrated in the following scenario: Sixteen-year-old Eric had been on vacation with his parents for 2 weeks and in another week would be going off to camp for 2 weeks. One day he approached his mother, saying, "It seems like I'm not getting any time at all to spend with my friends this summer. First I'm on vacation, and then I have to leave for camp. It's not like I don't want to go to camp, but I just wish it wasn't so soon and that I had more time to hang out with my friends." Eric's mother was tempted to jump in by saying something like "You should feel lucky that we can afford to send you to camp. Some kids don't even get to go on vacations. You should be glad that we can do such nice things for you. All you do during the year is hang out with your friends. A month away from them this summer isn't going to hurt you." Instead, she just nodded her head, said a few "I understands" and didn't offer any rebuttals. After he finished venting, he admitted that he knew nothing could be done about the situation because the money for camp couldn't be refunded and said that he really did want to go, but that it just seemed like a long time away from his friends.

The goal of active listening is to understand the other person's point of view. Understanding what is normal and what matters to children at various developmental stages makes it much easier to "walk in their shoes." Because Eric's mother realized that being with friends is so important to a 16-year-old, she was able to be more empathic.

Encouraging Communication

Even when parents try to use active listening, many complain that they just can't get their kids to open up, especially when they reach adolescence. Keep in mind that adolescents have a great need for privacy and will keep some of their thoughts and feelings to themselves because that is part of becoming independent. Resist the tendency to pry because the more you do that, the less they will share.

The following specific suggestions for opening up communication are appropriate for children of all ages.

1. Make time for communication

This is often easier said than done at today's hectic pace! However, try as much as possible to have at least several meals together each week and plan some type of family outing. With younger children, make bedtime a time to chat. Recognize that the older your children get, the more difficult it will be to do these things because of their busy schedules and desire to spend time with their friends. Nevertheless, it is generally not impossible to set aside some quality time on a weekend for at least one meal, and it is not unreasonable to expect that children and adolescents spend some time at home with other family members.

2. Don't force communication

If you sense that your child or adolescent is in a heightened state of arousal, reflect back what you see: "Gee, it looks like you had a bad day" or "You look happy. Something good must have happened." If you get no response or hear "Leave me alone," don't push. Chances are your child will talk when he or she is ready. Adolescents especially interpret the push for communication as a denial of their individuality and need for space.

3. Listen to how you say things

Open communication won't happen if you judge, criticize, use sarcasm, or start conversations with an "I suppose you got in trouble again" remark. In addition, tone of voice makes a world of difference in how a message comes across. It also helps to concentrate on talking less and listening more.

4. Respect your child's opinions

You don't have to agree with everything your child says, but above all you should honor his or her right to express an idea without being chastised or shut down. You also need to communicate that you expect the same in return.

While effective communication is essential in promoting healthy relationships, so are good discipline techniques. These are discussed in the following section.

THE WHAT'S AND WHY'S OF DISCIPLINE

"If you do that again, you'll be in *big* trouble."

"You'd better get those chores done, or you'll be grounded for 2 weeks."

"If you talk back to me again, you'll get your mouth washed out with soap."

Do any of these sound like things you heard from your parents when you were a child? Do any of them sound like things you have said to your own children? We would bet that they do sound familiar. Some of you might be tired of making threats such as these because it is hard to follow through on them, and, if you do, you don't feel good about the results.

Discipline is an inevitable and extremely important parenting function. The type of discipline you employ has a significant effect on the parent-child relationship. Although many parents assume that discipline is synonymous with punishment, in reality it is very different. Discipline is caring. It is teaching a better way. It is not intended to belittle or demean, but rather to help children learn appropriate behavior and to teach self-discipline, responsibility, and cooperation. The ultimate goal is to help children achieve confidence in their own ability to control themselves—not because they are afraid of what will happen if they don't but because they believe that they should behave appropriately.

There are lots of misconceptions about discipline. Did you know that:

Some discipline strategies promote prosocial behavior, self-control, and positive self-esteem, while others do not?

Most parents tend to use the discipline strategies that their own parents used with them?

A discipline strategy that is effective with one child may not be effective with another?

Discipline is most effective when it is conducted consistently and takes into consideration the child's age, experience, reasoning ability, and capacity for self-control?

A parent's choice of discipline techniques must also take into account the child's motives, aspirations, and fears?

Discipline needs to be directed at the child's specific misbehavior?

If parents have realistic expectations for their children, they are more likely to practice effective discipline?

Parents need to define clearly what is acceptable and unacceptable behavior for their children?

Adopting a new approach to discipline takes time, practice, reflection, and a lot of patience?

The temperament and maturity level of the parent and child influence whether conflict will or will not occur?

Your level of stress as a parent influences how you react to your children's misbehavior?

According to Hoffman (1970), discipline practices fall into three general categories: power assertion, love withdrawal, and induction. In *power assertion*, a parent uses spanking, slapping, hitting, shouting, scolding, criticizing, physically removing a child from a situation, inhibiting behavior, taking away the child's privileges or resources, threatening, or any combination of these measures. A parent who employs the *love withdrawal* approach expresses anger, disappointment, or disapproval; does not communicate with the child; and withdraws from the situation. A parent who uses *induction* gives explanations about why he or she thinks the child's behavior is wrong or inappropriate, pointing out the consequences of the child's behavior and tactfully appealing to the child's sense of mastery, fair play, or love of another person to redirect that child's behavior. An integral element of induction is the frequent expression of parental affection for the child.

Discipline Practices That Don't Work

Power Assertion

Many studies show power assertion to be ineffective. Parents who frequently use techniques of power assertion (e.g., physical punishment) produce children who exhibit high levels of aggression. A number of reasons might explain why power assertion leads to aggression in children. First, physical punishment frustrates children and creates further aggressive impulses. Second, parents who use physical punishment as discipline are modeling aggression for their children and teaching them undesirable ways to deal with frustration. Third, punishment itself is often a form of aggression and frequently invites another aggressive response. For example, as children misbehave, they provoke their parents into using physical control or engaging in power struggles with them. Children may respond to this situation by talking back, throwing tantrums, or doing something physical like hitting or kicking. The parents again use punishment, and a vicious cycle is in place.

While punishment may temporarily stop the misbehavior and offer immediate relief to the parent, it may also reinforce the parent's tendency to use coercive techniques again. Over time, it is likely that the punitive parent will punish the child more frequently and possibly with more intensity, creating a potentially abusive relationship.

Children whose parents frequently use power assertion become fearful of punishment, feel little guilt after harming others, and show poor self-control. Punishment promotes only momentary compliance, not lasting behavior change. Moreover, children learn to avoid the parent who punishes them, thus reducing the chances for the parent to teach socially acceptable behaviors.

In some cases, punishment is justifiable. When the behavior poses danger to the child or to others, such as running into the street or playing with fire, punishment may be in order. The timing, intensity, and consistency of the punishment—as well as the relationship between the punisher and child being punished—are all crucial elements in the effectiveness of punishment in stopping undesirable behavior. The immediate punishment of a child who runs into the street is considerably more effective than a delayed punishment. Firm punishment following such a dangerous behavior also makes the punishment more effective because it reduces the chances of that behavior happening again. A parent who is consistent in punishing a child for dangerous and highly undesirable behavior is more effective than an inconsistent parent. Finally, a parent who is usually warm and affectionate toward the child and who administers punishment only under special circumstances is significantly more effective than a parent who is generally cold or punitive toward the child.

Love Withdrawal

When a child does not behave in an acceptable manner, parents who use love withdrawal to discipline express a range of reactions—anger, disappointment, disapproval, or frustration. In addition, they frequently refuse to talk with the child and instead walk away from the situation. A teenager whose parents consistently use love withdrawal to discipline him put it this way: "When I misbehave, my mom gives me a nasty look and turns away." Another teenager said, "When I accidentally broke the vase on the kitchen table, my dad was furious. He wouldn't talk to me for 2 days. I just wanted to do anything to please him and make him talk to me again."

Love withdrawal as a disciplinary practice does very little to help children internalize control over their behavior. Although effective in bringing about compliance with adult expectations, love withdrawal increases children's need for approval and makes them fearful of expressing any pent-up emotions. Parental disapproval and disappointment do not necessarily teach children why they should refrain from a particular activity or how to correct an inappropriate behavior. Their sense of autonomy is not enhanced when they experience the high level of anxiety about external consequences associated with withdrawal of parental love.

DISCIPLINE PRACTICES THAT DO WORK

Induction

When parents use induction as a discipline practice, they point out the effects of the child's misbehavior on others. To help the child see such an effect, the parent might point out the physical consequences of the behavior by saying, "If you keep jumping on your sister's crib, it will break and she won't have a bed to sleep in" or "If you stay up late, you won't be able to stay awake and pay attention in school tomorrow." They may also point out affective consequences, such as "The reason I feel upset is that you have not done your chores yet" or "I am very unhappy because the bracelet you lost was very special to me." Giving clear and understandable explanations has been found to be offcctive with children as young as 2 years of age. It is effective because it teaches children how to behave so they can use what they learn in one situation in future situations. It permits them to think clearly enough to figure out what they should do in a given situation. Since parents point out the impact of their children's behaviors on others, this approach also promotes empathy. Empathy is a prerequisite to prosocial behavior, such as playing cooperatively with one's peers, sharing one's toys or games with playmates or schoolmates, and expressing sympathy for others.

When families use induction as a usual disciplinary practice, the family atmosphere is generally warm and accepting. Family members communicate openly and respectfully with one another and show concern and tolerance for others as well. The parents set firm, age-appropriate standards for behavior. As a result, the children grow up to be sociable, responsible, self-confident, and considerate of others. An additional advantage of induction is that it fosters higher levels of morality through empathy and caring for others.

In summary, the induction approach to discipline is designed to nurture self-esteem by demonstrating respect and instilling respect for the rights of others, encourage growth toward competence and independence, develop inner control or self-discipline by promoting the acceptance of blame for wrongdoing, promote effective verbal and reasoning skills, and build healthy attitudes toward authority.

Logical Consequences

The logical consequences approach to discipline, developed by the psychiatrist Rudolph Dreikurs, includes both a thinking and a learning component. According to Dreikurs and Soltz (1964), all misbehavior is the result of children's mistaken assumptions about how to "find a place" and gain status. Dreikurs cites four goals of misbehavior: to get attention, to gain power, to seek revenge, and to use disability to avoid doing something.

When children's goal is to get attention, they are under the impression that they only count when they are being noticed. If the goal is to gain power, they think they only count when they are dominating and manipulating the parents. Revengeful children think they can't be liked and don't have power but that they have a right to hurt others just as they have been hurt. Children who adopt the goal of inadequacy think they can't do anything right, so they won't try at all.

To use logical consequences effectively, you must first identify the child's goal. One way of doing this is to determine how you feel when your child does something you consider inappropriate. If you feel annoyed, the goal is probably to gain attention. If you feel angry and frustrated, as if you are in a win-lose situation, the goal is most likely power. If you feel hurt and personally attacked, the goal is probably revenge. If you feel hopeless and see that the child is discouraged and withdrawn, the goal is likely avoidance.

Another way of identifying goals is to observe the child's reactions when corrected. If the goal is to get attention, the child may stop misbehaving temporarily but will soon engage in another form of misbehavior of equal or greater intensity. Imagine, for example, a trip to the grocery store with a 5-year-old: The child first interrupts you as you are visiting with a friend, so you ask him please not to interrupt. Just a few minutes later, he starts pulling on your arm and begging you to finish the shopping.

If the goal is power, any attempt to stop the behavior will increase it. For instance, you may announce bedtime and notice that your youngster continues to sit in front of the television. You remind her again and hear "I'm not going to bed until this show is over." When you turn the television off and take her by the arm, she tries to pull away and get back to the television set.

If the goal is revenge, the child will continue the misbehavior and become violent if you attempt to stop it. With this goal, you will hear lots of yelling, screaming, and threatening, as well as physical acting out such as hitting or kicking. It is obvious that the revengeful child is very angry and wants to hurt you, physically or emotionally.

If the child's goal is avoidance, he or she will complete tasks very slowly and express lots of "I can't do its." Such children convey a sense of helplessness.

It is important to stress that logical consequences are not a form of punishment because they are directly related to the misbehavior and help children recognize their misbehavior as a mistake rather than a "sin." In addition, they teach children how to be more responsible for their behavior by allowing them to make choices to avoid negative consequences, and they don't involve threats or coercion. Finally, logical consequences deal with present behavior, whereas punishment is often an accumulation of all past wrongdoings. In employing logical consequences, it is important to be kind and firm, to avoid argument by stating the consequence succinctly, and to follow through with the consequence—generally, to talk less and act more.

Consequences are designed to be undesirable but never harmful. Logical consequences differ from natural consequences in that natural consequences result entirely from the child's own actions, as in the case of a child's putting a hand on a hot stove and getting burned. In employing logical consequences, parents arrange for children to experience the direct, unpleasant results of their own actions. If possible, the consequences should be clearly and firmly stated in advance so children know what will happen if they choose not to follow rules. For example, you might say, "I will be doing laundry this afternoon. If your clothes aren't in the basket when I am ready to start, you will need to be responsible for washing your clothes yourself." If the child fails to put the clothes in the basket, you *must* be consistent and follow through with the consequence, or your child will learn that you don't really mean what you say.

When employing consequences, you also need to take into account the age and capability of the child. Plainly, the example just given would not be appropriate for a 6-year-old. For a child this age, the parent could say that if the clothes aren't in the basket when it is time to do the laundry, the child will have to find other things to wear until the next time laundry is done.

When you give a consequence, state it in such a way that the child has a choice—either to continue to behave inappropriately or to change the behavior. For example, if your child is being disruptive at dinner, you can say, "If you aren't able to sit at the table and eat without playing with your food, you will have to leave the table. If you leave, you may come back and finish your dinner when you can behave properly." If your child promises to behave but a few minutes later is back to the same misbehavior, you can calmly say, "I'm sorry that you weren't able to behave. You will need to leave the table now." Another logical consequence for misbehavior at dinner is to say that there will be no dessert or snack after dinner if the child cannot finish the meal or behave appropriately.

Some parents are reluctant to use logical consequences because they are afraid of depriving their children. Children will not starve if they miss a few meals, and if you are consistent, they will quickly learn how to correct the situation. One parent shared the following as an example of an effectively delivered consequence:

My 9-year-old always liked to lean back in his chair during mealtime. Not only was this disruptive to the family, but it could have been dangerous for him. Warning him about the danger of this and getting angry when he did it accomplished nothing, so I decided to try logical consequences. I bought two metal extensions and put them on the front legs of the chair, which made the chair lean backward. During dinner, I noticed how uncomfortable he appeared, and after dinner he asked that the extensions be removed. I responded kindly but firmly that if he agreed to sit properly, I would remove them. However, if he did it again, he could expect that the extensions would be replaced until the behavior stopped.

Logical consequences teach children how to change their behavior. Parents must follow through, even though the consequence may inconvenience them somewhat or be distasteful to their children. If your goal is to change the behavior, remember that change won't occur overnight. However, if you are patient, firm, and consistent, you can avoid the power struggles and negative tactics that may be detrimental to the relationship.

Encouragement

Encouragement has important corrective influences for children. Dreikurs and Grey (1968) have stated, "Every misbehaving child is discouraged and needs continuous encouragement, just as a plant needs water and sunshine" (p. 47). To use encouragement effectively, parents must support their children's efforts to do well and to avoid trouble. They must also express acceptance of the child as worthwhile regardless of any deficiencies and believe in the child's abilities and assist him or her in developing new skills or capacities.

Encouragement helps children by providing them with good feelings about themselves, enhancing their sense of self-control, and bolstering their self-confidence. Your child will welcome your encouragement most when in danger of losing control or when he or she needs some extra support, positive words, or a renewed feeling of hope.

Keep in mind that encouragement is different from reinforcement. Encouragement is given before a task has begun or after the child fails. Reinforcement is a reward given after the child has successfully completed a task. Encouragement is best used when parents feel that the child's misbehavior is caused by disability as an excuse to avoid doing something. It is in these cases, when children are discouraged and self-doubting, that they need their parents to listen to them without judging or condemning.

Parents can master the art of encouragement by cultivating an encouraging frame of mind. In *The Encouragement Book,* written by Don Dinkmeyer and Lewis Losoncy (1980), an "encourager" is described as someone who listens effectively, focuses on the positive, is cooperative and accepting, uses humor and inspires hope, stimulates rather than humiliates, recognizes effort and improvement, is interested in feelings, and bases worth on "just being." These characteristics in a parent can provide a strong means of motivating the child.

No-Lose Method

The no-lose method developed by Gordon (1975) is helpful in resolving conflicts. It is used to resolve problems directly once the parent and child have understood each other. This approach to discipline builds on the active listening technique discussed earlier in this chapter. It presumes that both parents and children have relatively equal power and will work together on problem resolution until they find a solution acceptable to both.

The steps in the no-lose method are as follows:

1. Through active listening, the parent and child identify and define the problem or conflict.

2. Both parent and child generate possible alternative solutions.

3. The parent and child evaluate the possible consequences of each alternative.

4. The parent and child decide together on the best compromise. Both must allow and expect some give-and-take here.

5. Both think of concrete, explicit ways to implement the compromise.

6. After putting the solution into effect, both evaluate how it worked. If the solution has not worked, they consider the reasons why and try for a new solution.

The following scenario involving a 16-year-old girl who has repeatedly missed her 10:00 curfew show how the no-lose method might work in practice.

Parent: You were supposed to come home at 10:00, and it's now midnight. What happened?

(Parent allows child to talk and listens actively.)

Daughter: I just wasn't watching what time it was. That's all. I didn't mean to make you wait up for me.

(Parent responds to child's communication by expressing concern.)

Parent: When this happens, I wonder what might have happened to you. I especially wonder since you've done this before. How can we resolve this issue so it doesn't happen again?

(Parent invites child to generate a solution.)

Daughter: I can pay more attention to the time and set my watch alarm so it will alert me when it's time to go.

Parent: I like the second idea best. Let's give it a try. Now, we need to think of how we should deal with the possibility of your coming home late again.

(Parent discusses possible consequences with child.)

Daughter: You could not let me see my friends for a while.

Parent: That sounds reasonable to me.

If the daughter does not follow through with the solution generated, then the parent should enforce the agreed-upon consequence.

Reinforcement

Parents sometimes find that it is effective to use reinforcement techniques, especially in disciplining younger children. Briefly, reinforcement is anything that increases the frequency of a given behavior. To help a child who struggles to get good grades in school, dawdles over meals, or procrastinates about going to bed on time, some parents set up a reward system in which the child gets money for good grades, stickers for promptly eating meals, or a treat or surprise for getting to bed on time.

Although this technique can be very effective, many parents object to the use of rewards because they feel the child should be doing these things anyway. They also argue that by using rewards, the child may learn to do things only when there is a reward attached. These arguments certainly do have merit, but no matter how much we *think* children should be performing in certain ways, that doesn't mean they will. If you have tried other strategies that have failed, you might consider a reward system as an option.

In many cases, an effective reward serves as a temporary motivator to get a positive behavioral pattern established. Once such patterns start emerging, the ultimate goal becomes increasing the desirable behavior by encouragement alone, with the rewards slowly being phased out. (What you want to avoid is having your child refuse to do anything unless there is a reward attached.)

If you do use rewards, try to find things that really mean something to your child so he or she will think it is worth putting forth the effort. For example, if your 7-year-old loves to ride his bike, 15 extra minutes of riding time may be a good incentive for finishing a meal without dawdling. Other examples of rewards include special time with a parent or grandparent, a trip to the library, going on a picnic, or being able to do something special with a friend. If one of your goals is to have your children get along well without arguing and fighting, a family plan can be established whereby children earn points as a group for cooperating and getting along with one another. These points can be traded in for a special bedtime snack or a pizza party, for example. One family recently shared their success with "banking" points for cooperative behavior and trading them in for a trip to an amusement park. Obviously, this was a long-term project, but it was very effective because as they earned points each day they were allowed to mark off miles on the map. They could clearly see their progress, and there was an incentive to behave better the next day to earn more miles!

Loss of Privileges

Loss of privileges helps teach responsibility and is similar to logical consequences except that the lost privilege is not necessarily directly related to the misbehavior. For example, if children are arguing at the dinner table, parents might take away the privilege of playing with friends for the rest of the evening. As you can see, this loss is not directly related to arguing, but if the children value playtime with friends, it may be an effective way to teach more cooperative dinnertime behavior. With an adolescent who does not do assigned daily chores, taking away special privileges for a week might be effective.

Time-Out

Time-out is another effective technique for younger children. There are two types of time-out: In the first, the child is removed from the activity or setting for a short period of time (5 to 10 minutes). In the second, the child is allowed to stay where the activity is occurring but cannot participate. The time-out technique is most effective if the child is being removed from an activity that he or she likes because being removed from a preferred activity serves as an incentive for the child to correct the behavior in order to participate again. Parents can give children the choice to return from time-out when they are ready, or they can establish the time themselves. Giving the child the choice teaches more responsibility for self.

The following examples show how these two types of time-out can be used.

Method 1: Your two children are arguing over who gets to play with the blocks. You have asked them to play cooperatively, but they don't. You inform them, in a calm voice, that they will both need to go to their rooms until they think they can come back and play cooperatively. (If they come back and still can't play well together, you can try the time-out procedure again, or you can prohibit them from playing together for a longer period of time.)

Method 2: A group of neighborhood kids are playing in the yard. Your daughter is acting aggressively, so you remove her from the game to sit on the steps and watch until she can choose to go back to the game and play without pushing others around. (If she does return and continues to be aggressive, you will need to remove her from the setting.)

Time-out is also a good technique for helping children "cool down" and think about their behavior. Sometimes this is an effective technique for parents as well!

DISCIPLINE GUIDELINES FOR PARENTS OF ADOLESCENTS

Many parents find it much easier to discipline younger children than adolescents. For many reasons, what worked well with the 8-year-old will need significant modification for the 14-year-old.

The following suggestions should help as you revise your discipline techniques at the onset of early adolescence.

1. It is important to put difficulties in perspective by separating them into major and minor problems. Major problems could include stealing a car, abusing drugs or alcohol, or writing bad checks. Minor problems could be wearing clothes you don't approve of, having a messy room, or being 5 minutes late getting home.

2. Try to identify problems that have consequences for your teenager's life but not for yours. This is sometimes difficult to do because as a parent you think that all problems your adolescent experiences have consequences for your life. Remember that you can't take responsibility for everything and that it is best for your adolescent to learn now from the consequences of his or her actions. Examples of problems that don't affect you include not doing homework (when the teenager is capable of handling the work), skipping school, and not getting to work on time. You may argue that not doing homework affects your life because your teenager may not get a good job if he or she doesn't graduate from high school. You may need to convey that if the teen chooses to get bad grades, he or she should not expect to depend on you financially after high school. This type of message clearly spells out the consequences and allows the adolescent to make the choice. Some parents also worry that their adolescent's irresponsible behavior makes them look bad. It could, but the bottom line is that you can't live a person's life for him or her. Certainly, you should point out that you don't find the behavior appropriate, help the teen see the negative impact of the behavior, and indicate that you are available to help. By assuming this position, you no longer have to nag and threaten and engage in win-lose battles. Instead, you help your adolescent assume control over issues that he or she will need to be responsible for as an adult.

3. List the problems that your teenager has that affect both of you—for example, substance abuse, delinquent behavior, or staying out all night. Using "I" messages, communicate your feelings and concerns, and spell out the impact of the behavior for you and your teen.

Establish appropriate consequences or, if needed, seek counseling to address the underlying issues.

4. Eliminate triggers such as parental provocations, accusations, and a generally negative attitude toward the adolescent.

5. Take back responsibility for your own life. Too many parents sacrifice themselves so much for their adolescent that they build up resentment. In many cases, marriages and other relationships suffer. You will be a better parent if you acknowledge your own needs and take care of yourself, too.

6. Stand up for your own rights and well being. Use "I" messages when you want something from your teenager and be reasonable in what you request.

7. Follow through on your position. State clearly what you will do if you do not get cooperation and consideration. For example, if the clothes aren't picked up off the floor and put in the laundry, you won't do the laundry. If you ask your teen to do a favor or run an errand for you and he or she refuses to do it, refuse to do something the next time he or she asks. State refusals calmly: "I'm sorry, but I won't stay up to iron your shirt because you didn't take the garbage out for me when I asked."

8. Don't tolerate rudeness and disrespect. Inform your adolescent that you are a human being and deserve to be treated with respect. Don't raise your voice; firmly state how you expect to be treated. Remember, respect is a two-way street.

9. Your adolescent may try to persuade you to give money or privileges by badgering you, intimidate you by threatening to run away or never speak to you again, act like a martyr or give you the silent treatment if you deny or request something, or try the buttering-up act to get you to give in. Be alert! Recognize these tactics for what they are and try to remain firm and reasonable. Do not give in or allow yourself to become intimidated. Parents, not teenagers, should assume the authority in the family.

10. Remember that adolescents tend to get upset easily. A good rule of thumb is to try to avoid confrontations by staying calm. This is easier said than done: Close your eyes, take a deep breath, and count to 10 before you open your mouth!

CONCLUSION

When you were a young child, you might have learned the following jingle: "Stop, look, and listen before you cross the street. Use your eyes, use your ears, and then use your feet." Communication and discipline can be looked upon in much the same manner: Stop, use your eyes to see what is happening, and use your ears to hear what the issues are. Only after you have done these things should you begin to discuss the problem and determine the best way to deal with it.

Open and honest communication responds to children's underlying feelings and is the most effective way to discipline. Let the goal of your discipline be to prevent problems, to instill self-control, to teach and guide, to encourage appropriate behaviors, and to discourage and correct undesirable behaviors.

3

■■■■■■■■■■■■■■■■■■■■■■■■■■■■■■■

The Preschool Years

If you are the parent of a preschooler, you may sometimes wish that time would stand still so you could absorb the incredible number of changes that occur during this stage of development. As you watch your 4-year-old and her friend peddle their tricycles down the sidewalk, you reflect on the elaborate "pet store" they set up in the playroom before going outside to play. As the customer at this pet store, you had difficulty selecting your new pet from all the animals that sounded so alive as your daughter and her friend meowed, barked, and chirped! In addition to watching your preschool-age son enjoy real and imaginative play, you see him mesmerized as you read Dr. Seuss and Maurice Sendak. You are amazed at the new words he adds daily to his vocabulary, struggle with workable solutions to the "one more drink before bedtime" routine, and wonder how to respond to his challenge, "I'll do it myself."

The preschool years, ages 2 through 5, are a marked contrast from infancy and toddlerhood. It seems that almost overnight children change from communicating their needs by crying to verbally or behaviorally expressing their demands and desires. Instead of crawling or toddling, they are walking, skipping, and jumping. Their exuberance and energy enable them to explore their environment, and parents are often amused and amazed at the treasures their children discover!

Parents of preschoolers sometimes find themselves wondering how to help their children achieve the important tasks at this stage of development, identified by Hohenshil and Brown (1991, p. 8) as follows:

1. Developing a positive self-image

2. Enhancing social and emotional development

3. Encouraging independent thinking and developing problem-solving skills

4. Improving communication skills

5. Stimulating interest in the natural world

6. Increasing capability for self-discipline

7. Advancing the development of fundamental motor skills and abilities

8. Identifying special individual mental, social, and physical needs

9. Furthering the development of respect for the rights of others

10. Encouraging creativity

11. Giving and receiving sincere affection

CHARACTERISTICS OF PRESCHOOLERS

During this period of development, preschool-age children grow stronger and bigger physically and become more capable and independent psychologically and socially. They possess an abundant supply of energy and determination. They are very active: They play, run, talk to themselves and others, and investigate objects. As they get older, children volunteer to help do practically anything and everything around the house—cooking, cleaning, fixing things.

The primary developmental task during this period is developing autonomy and mastery. You will notice your preschooler gradually separating from you and learning to tolerate your absence. As this happens, he or she will want to be in control, do things alone, and be independent.

As a parent, you want your children to be independent so they learn self-control and how to care for themselves. To do this, they need to define and assert themselves as beings separate from you. As your children attempt self-assertion, they will initially act negatively or defiantly. They will struggle with emotional control and be caught between following their wishes and conforming to your parental demands. Their struggle may appear as temper tantrums, negativism (saying "No!"), and dawdling—all characteristics that have helped label this period "the terrible twos." Later, however, their negative behaviors turn into mature willfulness. They learn to care for themselves, dress, eat, toilet, and talk. They seek your discipline to help them behave acceptably.

As their behavior becomes more autonomous, preschoolers experience more accomplishments and a sense of mastery. They experiment, solve problems, and think using symbols. They also imitate sex-role behavior by playing the roles society defines for males and females. During this period, families can do a great deal to avoid sex-role stereotypes such as "Boys don't cry!" and "Girls are supposed to play with dolls." You can encourage preschoolers to engage in play activities based on what they like to do, not gender, and by allowing both boys and girls to express a full range of emotions.

The important goal for parents during this period is to foster and enhance their children's sense of autonomy and mastery. Children who are unsuccessful in achieving autonomy learn to feel shame and doubt. Shame results in feelings of self-consciousness, dependence, worthlessness, and incompetence. Self-doubt results when parents consistently restrict their children's attempts to experiment, explore, and gain mastery over their environment. Consequently, the children feel ineffectual, thwarted, and unable to learn about the environment. Thus, the more overprotective you are as a parent, the more dependent your children will become and the more difficulties they will have reaching their potential. On the other hand, when you encourage your children to be autonomous, they avoid internalizing shame and doubt and develop fewer negative feelings or behaviors, such as resentment and hostility.

Given their energy, exuberance, and curiosity, children in the preschool period need protection. Parents need to teach children about safety and explain why they cannot play with certain objects. Children's ability to climb, crawl, walk, and jump greatly increases their exposure to danger. It is the parents' job to anticipate children's activities inside and outside the home and to remove potential hazards, such as poisons.

In this chapter, we will explore more about the world of the preschool child by focusing on five areas of development: physical, intellectual, self-, social, and emotional. Each of these areas includes discussion of a typical problem and recommendations for dealing with it.

PHYSICAL DEVELOPMENT

By the time children are 2 years old, they've quadrupled their birth weight. If your child's growth rate at infancy were to continue, you would end up with a giant! Fortunately, the rate of physical growth slows down considerably in early and middle childhood. Children grow only 2 to 3 inches and gain only 5 to 7 pounds in weight each year throughout the entire preschool period. As your preschooler grows older, the percentage of increase in his or her height and weight decreases with each year. You will also notice that body proportion and muscle-to-fat ratio undergo dramatic change during the preschool years. The top-heavy, chubby infant gradually becomes more slender and longer legged. If your child is a girl, she will have slightly more body fat than a boy.

It is important to remember the many individual differences in physical growth. Same-age children grow at different rates and differ greatly in physical size. Each body system has its own unique, carefully timed pattern of maturation. Both heredity and environment influence these differences.

One of the developmental tasks of the toddler period, which precedes the preschool years, is enhancement or refinement of locomotion. Toddling occurs mostly during the second year of life. The toddler's waddle changes into a graceful walk by about age 3. With a refined, comfortable walk, children add more skills to their movement repertoire, beginning with running and jumping. By age 4, children gain still more physical abilities, such as hopping on one foot and skipping.

Running skills also improve, and this lets children play many games that require running. You will notice, however, that your child's speed and gait are still a bit awkward, hampered by short legs and arms that aren't in sync with the rest of the running gait.

Parents can help their children gain physical skills by exposing them to various forms of movement, such as swimming, roller skating, sledding, and tricycle riding. The tricycle (and later the bicycle) gives children a special joy because by riding it they can show mastery over an object as well as gain independence.

Riding a tricycle is also a way to experience a thrill and have playtime alone or with friends.

The chart on the following pages summarizes a number of gross and fine motor skills that change during the preschool years. The information here can be a rough guide to your child's motor and perceptual development. Although the tasks listed are normally accomplished by 75 to 80% of the children at the designated age levels, it is important to stress that each child will develop at his or her own rate. If you see your child failing to master four to six of the tasks for his or her age, you may want to consider asking your pediatrician to refer you to someone who can do a more thorough evaluation and offer ideas of what can be done if your child needs help.

As a parent, you know how important eating habits are to the young child. Eating habits become ingrained early in life. The healthier eating course you start your children on, the healthier they are likely to be. What children eat affects their skeletal growth, body shape, and susceptibility to disease. An unbalanced diet results in below-average physical development, which depresses the body's immune system, making children more susceptible to disease. Preschoolers require between 1,400 to 1,800 calories a day and should avoid meals with excessive fat, protein, carbohydrates, or sugar.

Besides nutrition, other factors affect children's emotional well being—large doses of love and affection, relative freedom from disease, nonpolluted environments, exercise, and heredity. While it is true that genes play a major role in growth by influencing the body's production and sensitivity to hormones, a healthy, loving environment also helps children reach their genetic potential.

A Typical Physical Development Problem: Finicky Eating

It's dinnertime, and your 3½-year-old child is not eating much. He sits and plays with his food, ignoring your pleas to eat. You are concerned because he has been a good eater. You wonder why he has suddenly become so finicky and why there are certain foods he absolutely refuses to taste. You also are puzzled because he instantly becomes hungry when candy is offered. You have tried cajoling, rewarding with a treat, and playing games to get him to eat, but your efforts have failed, and you're getting quite frustrated. No matter what you do, he doesn't eat much at mealtime.

Gross and Fine Motor Skills during the Preschool Years

Ages 2 through 3   Yes   No

1. Displays a variety of scribbling behaviors. ☐ ☐

2. Can walk rhythmically at an even pace. ☐ ☐

3. Can step off a low object, one foot ahead of the other. ☐ ☐

4. Can name hands, feet, head, and some face parts. ☐ ☐

5. Opposes thumb to fingers when grasping objects and releases objects smoothly from finger-thumb grasp. ☐ ☐

6. Can walk a 2-inch wide line placed on ground for 10 feet. ☐ ☐

Ages 4 through 4½   Yes   No

1. Can forward broad jump, both feet together and clear of ground at the same time. ☐ ☐

2. Can hop two to three times on one foot without precision or rhythm. ☐ ☐

3. Walks and runs with arm action coordinated with leg action. ☐ ☐

4. Can walk a circular line a short distance. ☐ ☐

5. Can draw a crude circle. ☐ ☐

6. Can draw a simple cross using a vertical and horizontal line. ☐ ☐

Ages 5 through 5½   Yes   No

1. Runs 30 yards in just over 8 seconds. ☐ ☐

2. Balances on one foot (girls 6 to 8 seconds/ boys 4 to 6 seconds). ☐ ☐

3. Catches large playground ball bounced to him or her chest-high from 15 feet away, four to five times out of five. ☐ ☐

Ages 5 through 5½ (continued)	**Yes**	**No**

4. Draws rectangle and square one side at a time instead of as a continuous line. ☐ ☐

5. Can high jump 8 inches or higher over bar with simultaneous two-foot takeoff. ☐ ☐

6. Bounces playground ball, using one or two hands, a distance of 3 to 4 feet. ☐ ☐

Note. From *Psychomotor Behavior in Education and Sport* (pp. 61– 64) by B. J. Cratty, 1974, Springfield, IL: Charles C Thomas. Adapted by permission of the author.

Why do you have a finicky eater, and what can you do about this problem?

1. Realize that part of finicky eating may be a normal decline in your child's appetite. The decline has to do with the slow physical growth typical at this time. Beginning at about age 2, children undergo a dramatic change in both the quantity and variety of foods they eat. As a result, they become picky eaters.

2. Understand that wariness of different foods may indicate that your child is still learning about food— which food is and is not safe to eat. (By sticking to familiar foods, children know they won't swallow something dangerous.)

3. Recognize that your child's internal hunger cues may not necessarily follow your schedule. You may need to be flexible and willing to accommodate the change in your child's eating patterns. For example, if your child gets hungry for dinner as it gets dark, be willing to serve his or her meal at this time.

4. Try a reward system for eating at mealtime. Many parents rely on sweets, but this has negative consequences. Sugar consumption may contribute to dental cavities and obesity. If you do use candy as a reward for eating, use it sparingly and in a controlled amount. Also, avoid giving candy or allowing children to eat candy before meals. An alternative to candy is a sticker chart

for finishing the meal. Kids at this age like stickers, and parents find them a good motivator.

5. Use logical consequences: "If you can't eat your food without playing with it, you will need to go to your room. If you decide to come back and finish your supper, then you can have your treat." Be sure to stick to your guns and not let your child have a treat if he or she doesn't finish the meal! If you give in, you will continue to have a finicky eater.

6. If you think your child isn't getting needed nutrients, try giving smaller amounts and require at least a taste or two of each type of food.

7. Remember, your child's finicky eating won't last forever. As a matter of fact, you may wish that your child would be a bit more finicky when adolescence approaches and you get eaten out of house and home!

INTELLECTUAL DEVELOPMENT

Do the following statements sound familiar?

"I'm not going to sleep in my room because there is a monster in the closet."

"Ten pennies are better than a dime."

"When I went for a walk, the sun followed me."

These statements reflect some of the ways preschoolers think and reason. Between ages 2 and 5, children begin to represent their actions mentally, to anticipate consequences before an action actually occurs, and to develop some idea of cause and effect. They see their actions as a means to the end, ways of achieving desired goals.

The famous developmental psychologist Jean Piaget (1950) divided young children's intellectual development into two substages: The first (ages 2 through 4) is called *preconceptual;* the second (ages 4 through 7) is called *intuitive*. In the preconceptual substage, children begin to internalize objects and events in their environments and to develop concepts about them. Developing concepts enables children to classify and identify objects in their world. For example, children are able to recognize a dog because they have the notion that a dog is something that walks on four legs, has fur and long ears, and barks. However, children may have difficulty distinguishing among things belonging to the same category. For example, a child who sees one dog may think it is the same one he or she saw before. The child simply fails to recognize that similar objects, animals, or individuals can retain identities of their own.

Piaget also noted two other features of the preconceptual substage that can help parents understand their children's intellectual development. One of these features, referred to as *transductive reasoning*, is when a child reasons from a particular event to another event rather than in a cause-and-effect manner. For example, a child at this age may think it gets dark at night so he or she can go to bed or believe that every bank teller is nice because one bank teller gave him or her candy. The other intellectual feature, referred to as *syncretic reasoning*, characterizes the child's inconsistent use of rules. When asked to group objects that belong together, a child might group a blue crayon, a blue truck, and a blue animal because they are all blue. Or the child might group a marble and a ball together and then throw in a pencil just because it is the same color as the ball or marble. At this age, children do not use the same rule consistently, which explains why it is difficult for younger preschoolers to play a game with rules. You certainly can play and enjoy the game as long as you are willing to tolerate the creative, natural, and spontaneous rule bending!

In Piaget's second substage, intuitive thinking, the child's thoughts are based on immediate comprehension rather than on logical processes. In solving a problem, the child may rely on what he or she hears or sees rather than reasoning about the problem logically.

Intuitive thinking poses a number of difficulties, including inability to classify objects, inability to take another's perspective, and overreliance on perception. You can use the following experiment to assess whether a child knows how to classify: Show the child a collection of 12 objects, such as toys. In this collection there should be two subclasses—for example, 7 blocks and 5 trucks. Tell the child that these objects are toys of two different types—trucks and blocks. Next ask if there are more blocks than toys. Listen to the response. The child might say, "There are more blocks." This answer reflects the child's incomplete understanding of classes. You may even notice older children having difficulty with this simple problem.

Children's inability to take into account another's point of view, known as *egocentrism*, is demonstrated when they claim that the sun or moon is following them. Likewise, when talking on the telephone with a relative, your child might answer the relative's questions by nodding or shaking his or her head, totally oblivious to the bewilderment of the relative at the other end of the line. This inability to entertain another person's view is also evident in conversations with other children. You might have heard children "conversing" by taking turns talking but not paying much attention to their listeners or to other speakers. Consider the following:

Ryan: I like ice cream.

Jessica: It's raining.

Ryan: My favorite is vanilla ice cream.

Jessica: I like my umbrella.

Ryan: I also like chocolate ice cream.

In addition, *perception* dominates children's thinking at this stage. As a result, they make judgments based on the immediate, perceptual appearance of objects in their environment. For example, if children are shown two identical balls of modeling clay, they will acknowledge that there is the same amount of clay in each ball. If the shape of one ball is elongated into a hot-dog shape, they will believe the hot-dog shape contains more clay. In this situation, it is clear that they have relied on their perception of the altered ball of clay rather than on logical rules, which will characterize thinking in the school years. This example also demonstrates how preschool children focus on one aspect of a situation and neglect other important features. Children at this age are not yet able to think through a series of steps and then reverse direction, returning to the starting point.

For parents, there are some advantages to the young child's intellectual limitations. If your child complains about getting a small pancake, for example, cut it in smaller pieces and spread it around; your child will now believe that it is much bigger!

Two other aspects characterize preschoolers' thinking: animism and artificialism. *Animism* is when children think that nature or natural objects are conscious, just as people are. This is why they pick up a doll and comfort it when it falls or think cars are alive because they move. *Artificialism* describes the belief that someone causes or creates natural phenomena. For example, preschoolers might explain that the sun is a fire set by someone lighting a match or that rain falls because fire fighters are spraying water from the sky. Preschoolers will demonstrate animism and artificialism when asked questions such as the following:

What are clouds made of? Where do they come from?

Why do people get sick?

Are bicycles alive? How do you know?

Why can we only see stars at night?

Where does the sun go at night?

Both animism and artificialism allow children to engage in make-believe play, one of the most fascinating aspects of this period of development. Imaginary friends may be frequent guests at your table, accompany your children on outings, and probably assume the blame for much misbehavior! As you listen to the conversations with imaginary friends or observe your child's play scenes, you probably see a lot of your present-day reality reflected in the play. For example, after a trip to a museum, a preschooler might come home and set up a museum in the living room. Imaginary play helps stimulate the child's thinking and enhances his or her ability to understand the feelings of others. This awareness helps develop social competence.

Besides creating imaginary friends and playing make believe, children at this age may assume different identities. They may act like an animal or become an entirely different person—maybe Frank, a friend of the family. As a parent, you are never sure to whom you are speaking—your daughter (alias Fido) or your son (alias Frank)! Children at this age may insist that you play with them in carrying out the role: A plate becomes a dog bowl; your car becomes Frank's jeep.

Language is another aspect of intellectual development at this period. At age 2, the average child has a vocabulary of more than 50 words. The child begins to join words into two- and three-word phrases. This represents a definite increase in verbal communication skills and interest in language. At about 2½ years of age, you are likely to see new words added every day. Children definitely try to communicate at this age, become frustrated when they can't make themselves understood, and sometimes drive their parents crazy because they ask so many questions. Questions are an important way for them to learn, and they increase their understanding and their vocabulary as they listen to your explanations. Remember that children do understand most of what is said to them, particularly as they reach the end of the preschool years. At approximately age 3, children's vocabulary increases to around 1,000 words. Most of what they communicate is intelligible even to strangers. By age 4, the average child's language is well established.

Parents can facilitate language development by reading to their children, by talking and labeling objects in daily activities, and by encouraging children to talk by asking questions and engaging them in conversations

A Typical Intellectual Development Problem: Childhood Fears

Consider the following situation: It is not Halloween, but your 4-year-old is suddenly afraid to go to bed at night because she insists there are monsters in her room. Despite your assurances, she continues to believe these creatures are real and might hurt her. She refuses to go to bed alone. When you tell her there are no monsters in the house, she insists they were there last night. She will go to bed only if you stay in the room with her. You reluctantly give in and sit by her bed until she goes to sleep, but after several nights of doing this, you are getting very frustrated.

Children's difficulty distinguishing between reality and fantasy can contribute to the development of fears of monsters, ghosts, or the bogeyman. As a parent, what can you do when your preschooler is afraid to go to bed or play in a certain spot because there might be monsters or other creatures there?

1. Don't ridicule or tease about the fears. Remember that fear of monsters or other creatures is very normal at this age. For the preschooler, everything is real: It is difficult at this age to distinguish between fantasy and reality. Your child will outgrow fears of monsters when he or she is developmentally able to tell the difference between fantasy and reality.

2. Help find a solution that makes the child feel more powerful than the monster. For example, he or she could make a scary mask to hang on the door to frighten the monster away. Or the child could take an empty spray bottle, label it "monster repellent," and use it to pretend to spray the room before going to bed each night (Vernon, 1993).

3. Buy a night-light or a large flashlight. While children at this age believe monsters exist, they also think a night-light drives them away.

4. Read stories that dispel the myth of monsters, such as *There Is a Monster under My Bed* (Howe, 1986) or *How to Deal with Monsters* (Powell, 1990).

5. Monitor television viewing so the child doesn't watch scary shows, especially just before bedtime.

SELF-DEVELOPMENT

Do you ever get frustrated when you are trying to go somewhere and your preschooler is following a different timetable? Do you get impatient when your child waits until the last minute to get dressed for preschool, then wastes even more time by insisting on wearing certain clothes? These issues are typical of the general theme that runs across this critical preschool period—the development of a sense of autonomy. Beginning at about age 2, children become aware of their separateness. Preschoolers often cherish their emerging sense of independence by becoming nay-sayers, by insisting that things be done their way, and by following a rigid set of rituals, such as having two stories at bedtime, certain toys in the tub during bath time, or sitting at a particular place during meals. Perhaps this is why the initial part of this period is often called the "terrible twos." Parents and children often end up in a battle of wills. When parents don't give in, children may express their displeasure in a variety of ways, including throwing tantrums.

Children let their parents know in more ways than one that the children's routines ought to be followed precisely. It helps to be sensitive to your child's messages and to understand that your child's rituals serve a number of purposes. Rituals bring control and order to your child's environment and provide a sense of stability and predictability.

The phrase "I can do it myself" reflects the dominant theme of this stage. Children like to do things on their own and derive a great deal of pleasure and pride from their accomplishments. The positive results of their independent achievements strengthen their sense of autonomy. Children begin to view themselves as competent and capable of satisfying their own needs. It is therefore very important for parents to provide opportunities for their children to do things on their own, such as dressing themselves, cleaning their own rooms, and helping with jobs around the house. The more you allow your child to experience autonomy, the more likely he or she will develop self-confidence and begin to take appropriate risks.

Children pursue their quest for autonomy with an endless supply of energy and an incredibly high level of persistence. When they initiate a particular task, they tend to stick to the task until they have mastered it. It is not uncommon for preschoolers to vehemently refuse any adult help, so adults might not want to interfere or offer their assistance until they are asked. It is also a good idea to let children help around the house, even though in the process of helping, children may break things or create more mess. Although it is usually easier to do something yourself, this is an important way for children to learn skills. Patience and encouragement on your part will pay off for your child in the long run.

Continual parental discouragement and criticism only add to children's feelings of failure, shame, and self-doubt. As a result, children expect to fail at whatever they do. They refrain from trying all kinds of new activities, which means they aren't gaining new skills. Later, self-doubting children become comfortable only in highly structured situations where the risk of failure is minimal.

Another mechanism that shapes preschoolers' sense of autonomy is imitation. If you have older children, you may remember hearing them imitate you scolding the dog or rounding up the kids for bed. Beware! Your child will readily imitate you, so you may want to monitor what you say and do—it will come back to haunt you. Children at this age don't miss much, so don't be too surprised at what you hear coming out of their mouths.

Developing initiative is another hallmark of the preschool period. As children move out into the social world, they face increasing challenges. They are expected to assume more and more responsibility—for their bodies, behavior, toys, pets. In turn, they increase their self-initiated behaviors. Children also begin to develop a conscience, which serves as a source of self-observation, self-guidance, and self-punishment. If their self-initiated actions bring more punishment than reward, they feel bad. Parents need to understand the importance of this sense of initiative and encourage it by giving children the freedom and opportunity to do their own physical activities (running or jumping), intellectual activities (asking questions or telling stories), and social activities (play).

Self-control is another major aspect of self-development during the preschool years. As children mature, it becomes easier for them to comply with requests, adapt their behavior to a given situation, postpone action, and behave in socially acceptable ways. Thus, self-control in preschoolers takes the form of not only increasing ability to control objects and events in the environment but also the ability to control their own impulses.

As children get older, they become less frustrated and more tolerant when their wishes or needs are not met immediately. A rudimentary sense of time, which emerges somewhere between ages 2 and 3½, helps them tolerate delays more easily. This is not to say that parents won't sometimes be overwhelmed by questions such as "Can I have this now?" or "When are we going to eat? I'm hungry now!" Parental responses to these frustrations are important. Parents can help their children by teaching them some self-control strategies. For example, if you are riding in the car and your children are continually bombarding you with the "Are we there yet?" question, you could draw a simple map with some significant landmarks—maybe a church, a school, a red house, and a white house. Have the children look at the map and the scenery to give them an idea of when they might be there. You can also acknowledge that it is hard to wait and praise them for being patient when they are sitting quietly in the car, at the doctor's office, or elsewhere.

A related self-development issue is how preschoolers view themselves. As noted previously, they are very egocentric, assuming that the world revolves around them. It is difficult for them to see things from another's perspective. This egocentrism is also reflected in their self-descriptions. In concrete ways, they describe their physical appearance, what they own, what they do, and what they like. The excessive use of "my" and "mine" during this period is interpreted by many child development professionals as a way children mark off boundaries between themselves and others. If children have disagreements and are possessive over toys, for instance, they are in many respects asserting their individuality and selfhood. But parents get tired of hearing these disagreements. If a dispute occurs over a toy, it might help parents to say to the possessive child, "I know the toy is yours, but I want you to let someone else play with it for a while."

For the most part, preschoolers have high self-esteem. As a matter of fact, you will find they overrate their abilities and underestimate the difficulty of tasks at hand. In the view of preschoolers, nothing is impossible! This high sense of self-esteem is advantageous because there are so many skills to master at this age. With each mastery, the sense of initiative and competence increases. Parental patience and encouragement enhances this sense of competence. It is not until children enter school and begin comparing their performance to others' that self-esteem declines.

A Typical Self-Development Problem: Willful Behavior

If you have experienced an episode like the following one with a 2-year-old, you are not alone:

Parent: Please put on your coat.

Child: No!

Parent: It's time to go now. Come on!

Child: No! I don't wanna go!

Parent: I'll leave without you then!

Child: *(Shows no signs of putting on the coat.)*

Many parents feel irritated that their child says no to every-thing. For some parents, negative behavior becomes the major focus of discipline, especially for 2- and 3-year-olds. Even though you may know this is the stage where children are becoming autonomous and independent, you may still not understand why your child has to say no to almost every request! His or her behav-ior probably stretches the limits of your patience. In response, you may become stern or angry. Some parents are frightened by the anger and frustration they feel over their child's willful behavior.

Keep in mind that saying no is children's way of asserting themselves and dominating others. It is their way of separating from parents and developing personal competence. As they do so, children are oblivious to the reactions of others; they will continue their willful behavior despite parents' rising blood pressure. It is important to remember that children act this way because they are egocentric—they understand the world only from their own perspective. They think that everyone thinks as they do, and they cannot imagine what adults are thinking.

The following specific suggestions will help you deal more effectively with this type of behavior in your child.

1. Understand that your child's "No!" is not a defiant testing of your authority. The preschool period is a time when children spontaneously take initiative and develop a sense of autonomy. In this process, they test their limits. If parents do not clearly define limits, children will just keep on testing. If restricted, they are likely to engage their parents in a battle of wills.

2. Do not overreact. Offer your child an opportunity to assert his or her will within reasonable limits. If you are getting ready to go somewhere and don't want your child's refusals to delay you, offer a choice by saying, "It's time to go to the library. Do you want to

wear your yellow sweater or green jacket?" This word-ing does not encourage a "No!" response and gives your child an opportunity to make a choice and assert selfhood.

3. Avoid yes-or-no questions. "Would you like to go to the library now?" will almost always elicit a "No!" response from your child. Instead, use clear, action-oriented statements to convey your expectations, then allow a choice. An example would be "It's time for bed now. Which book do you want me to read?" This method will help divert your child's attention to another object or activity and make your child forget the "No!" response.

4. Praise your child when he or she does not display a negative response.

5. Make things into a game. For example, while getting ready to leave the house, you can say, "Let's see if you can have your jacket on by the time I count to 10."

SOCIAL DEVELOPMENT

Pointing to his curved piece of wood, a 4-year-old said to his friend, "My horse is bigger and faster than yours!" Referring to the plastic pot over her head, his friend said, "But my hat is bigger than your hat!" In response, the boy said, "So what? I have a whole bunch of big hats at home."

As this example illustrates, peers and play are two dominant and necessary contributors to the preschooler's social development. Playing with peers takes up an increasing amount of time during early childhood. In addition to parents, peers become another source of information and feedback; they also function as a source of comparison and influence one another's play.

In families with more than one child, siblings become major participants in the preschooler's social activities. As siblings interact, sometimes they play cooperatively. At other times they play aggressively. According to Seifert and Hoffnung (1993), these interactions help develop social understanding and enable the preschooler to grasp the particular feelings, intentions, and needs of others. Older siblings may act as role models by teaching their younger sisters or brothers social skills and parental expectations. However, if an older sibling feels a need to outshine a preschool-age sibling, the preschooler may be discouraged from developing certain social skills. Therefore, parents need to recognize and respond appropriately to the social needs of all of their children

In addition to engaging in play with siblings, preschoolers interact quite a bit with peers. Most of their interactions revolve around play. This increases their associations with others, provides a chance to explore the environment, allows them to engage in a variety of behaviors, helps relieve tension, and encourages language development and creativity.

Sigmund Freud (1974) referred to play as the child's first cultural and psychological achievement. If you watch children's play, you will discover that play is their language. It is their way of communicating, of mastering the world, and of asserting themselves. You will notice that play forms a link between their inner and outer worlds as they demonstrate what they know or guess about the world.

Children use different types of play—solitary, onlooker, parallel, associative, and cooperative. In solitary play, the child plays alone and independently of other children. It is common for 2- and 3-year-olds to play in this manner, seemingly careless of what others around them are doing. Onlooker play takes place when a child watches other children playing. The child may initiate a conversation with or ask a question of the other children but does not participate in their play. A child in parallel play also plays alone but plays with a similar toy or imitates the manner of play of other children. Associative play occurs when the child seems to be more interested in associating with other children than in the play task itself. This explains why a child at this stage may willingly lend a toy or follow another child in line. In cooperative play, a group of children engage in an organized activity, such as hide-and-seek or a game organized at preschool by the teacher.

Expect 2- to 3-year-olds to engage in solitary, onlooker, and parallel play. Four- and 5-year-olds are more likely to be involved in associative and cooperative play. At the end of the preschool years, a child engages most often in cooperative play.

Preschoolers' social development also includes distinguishing between their own and others' intentional and accidental behaviors. Two-year-olds use words that announce intentions, such as "gonna" and "wanna." By age 3, the child begins to understand whether the actions of others are intentional or accidental. At first, though, children match words with actions to judge intentionality rather than relying on other ways of interpreting actions.

In other words, if a person says he or she is going to do a particular thing and then does it, the child judges the action to be
intentional. If action does not follow the words, the preschooler
presumes the other person did not intend to do what was promised.
By the end of the preschool period, around age 5, children use a
broader variety of cues to judge other people's intentions.

Preschoolers' ability to understand intentions is vital to their
social and emotional development. The more they can separate
deliberate from accidental acts, the easier it is for them to interpret others' behavior and respond to it appropriately. If they
have this understanding, they will be less likely to become angry
and retaliate if, for example, someone accidentally knocks down
the block tower they are building. Preschoolers who can make
accurate judgments about others' actions seem to get along better
with their peers.

A Typical Social Development Problem: Sibling Rivalry

Your two young children are at it again. They are picking on each
other, disrupting the household. Concerned that they could hurt
each other, you intervene and hear: "He started it!" "Na-ah! She did!"

Aggressive behaviors, including sibling rivalry, are a common
occurrence during the preschool period. Sibling rivalry is a univer-
sal phenomenon. It usually involves one child's negative feelings
toward a brother or a sister because of competition or jealousy.
It occurs when the child's need to feel worthwhile is frustrated
or when the child tries to do better than a sibling. The child acts
out negative feelings through verbal or physical aggression.

What do you do in these kinds of situations? First of all, try to
prevent them by acknowledging each child for his or her individual
accomplishments. This prevents jealousy from developing. Second,
provide each child with his or her own time for love and affection.
This is especially crucial when a new baby is added to the family.

Here are some specific suggestions for dealing with sibling
rivalry after it happens.

1. Use a time-out procedure by placing the children in
   separate rooms or having them sit on separate chairs
   for a short time. This cooling-down period can range
   from 2 to 15 minutes depending on the severity of the
   fighting.

2. Avoid being partial; make no attempts to determine
   who is to blame for a fight. Discourage the children

from arguing with you and from baiting each other into starting another fight. Be consistent in your use of this approach.

3. Praise your children when they play cooperatively with each other.

4. Model positive ways of dealing with conflict, such as talking about the issue calmly, listening, and reaching a resolution. Children learn more from your actions than from your words.

5. Use positive reinforcement. Make a chart to post on the refrigerator. For each hour the children go without fighting, reward them with a sticker. Determine how many stickers they need before they each can earn a special non-candy treat, an activity, or a small prize from a surprise box of inexpensive trinkets.

6. If a child routinely and consistently shows aggressive behavior that inflicts psychological or bodily harm to a sibling, consider psychological counseling for the child.

EMOTIONAL DEVELOPMENT

Preschoolers' ability to represent events mentally, their enhanced language skills, and their increasing self-awareness play a major role in emotional development. During these years, preschoolers develop a better understanding of their own and others' feelings and become more capable of controlling their emotions.

Although their vocabulary is expanding, preschoolers are still rather limited in expressing how they feel. As a result, they will often express feelings behaviorally. For example, you may see children jump up and down if they are excited or happy, throw a tantrum if they are frustrated, or kick and scream if they are angry. It is important that parents look beyond the behavior to determine what children might be feeling. If the parents identify and acknowledge these feelings, children can learn to express them verbally.

As they get older, preschoolers' ability to think about their own and others' behavior increases, and their language begins to demonstrate their understanding of their own feelings and the feelings of others. By the end of the preschool period, they are better able to tell you, for example, why a friend is upset and doesn't want to participate in an activity. Children at this age also begin responding verbally or physically to others' emotions by hugging, kissing, or giving toys. However, their understanding of other people's emotions is limited by their perceptions. They tend to focus on the most obvious aspects of an emotional situation, such as being sad, happy, or mad.

How to behave emotionally is an important aspect of development at this age. By watching others, children learn how to control their expressions of emotion, especially anger. Though parents sometimes do not care for its expression, anger is essential to the child's developing sense of autonomy. Children rely heavily on their parents to learn how to express anger appropriately. Because children imitate their parents' behavior, parents need to be good role models. If children see their parents expressing anger in a controlled manner and avoiding yelling, hitting, or shoving, they will be less likely to be out of control in their own expression of anger.

Sometimes children this age use anger to get attention. If you sense this is the case, ignore the angry expressions if they don't harm others. If the child doesn't get attention, there's no incentive to continue the angry outbursts. You can also help your child see what happens when he or she takes anger out on others. For example, you could use puppets to demonstrate a fight in which one puppet gets hurt, then ask your child how the hurt puppet feels.

In addition to anger, parents of preschoolers will also recognize that their children experience self-conscious feelings of embarrassment, coupled with shyness. These feelings are obvious in the young child who hides his or her head behind a security blanket or peeks out at a stranger from behind a parent's legs. These are very normal emotions at this period, as are fears—of strangers, the dark, new situations, and things that go "bump" in the night.

A Typical Emotional Development Problem:
Temper Tantrums

Imagine a 3-year-old so angry and frustrated that he loses control and throws himself on the floor, screaming and kicking. Sometimes he holds his breath until he is blue. This child's temper tantrums really distress his parents because they feel frustrated and helpless. Because the parents don't know how to stop the tantrums, they give in to the child's demands, inadvertently reinforcing the tantrum behavior. Sometimes the parents resort to threats: "If you do that again, I will take your toy away" or "If you stomp your feet one more time, you'll be sent to your room."

Does all this sound familiar? Occasional temper tantrums are common around the age of 2 but may continue to be normal for 3- and 4-year-olds. Tantrums are a way of dealing with frustration. However, frequent tantrums in children over age 4 may signify a more serious problem in the child or the parents' lack of effective methods in dealing with the problem. What can you do about tantrums?

1. Use a brief time-out, described in chapter 2, until the anger simmers down. Time-out is most effective when you can remove the child from a favorite activity.

2. Assuming the child isn't in danger, leave him or her alone. Walk away or simply grit your teeth and ignore it. Without an audience, a tantrum isn't as much fun!

3. Stand firm and do not concede to your child's wishes. For example, if your child throws a fit at the grocery store checkout counter because he or she can't have a candy bar, explain that you are sorry but that you will not buy the candy. You will have to deal with your embarrassment if the child continues to throw a fit, but if you give in you will reinforce the negative behavior. Remember, other parents go through this, too.

4. Consistently praise the child for appropriate behavior.

5. Remember that tantrums are a fantastic way to control. In chapter 1 we discussed the permissive parent and the parent with low frustration tolerance. Such parents may believe it is easier to give in than put up with misbehavior. That may be true in the short term, but preschoolers who learn to use tantrums to get their way often resort to similar behaviors as teenagers— and then the problem escalates.

CONCLUSION

If your children are no longer preschool age, you may have forgotten some of the wonderfully idiosyncratic behaviors that characterize this period of development. And if you are the parent of a preschooler, you have lots to cherish! This is an amazing period because children learn so much, are excited about life, and experience everything with vigor.

Capture the moment because as children get older, they won't carry on conversations with their imaginary playmates, be fascinated by nursery rhymes, or learn to put words together in coherent sentences. They will graduate from tricycle to bicycle riding, and before you know it, their wheels will be in the form of a car! They may never again explore their surroundings with as much curiosity, nor feel as awestruck by their discoveries. They will never be as innocent or unpretentious as they are at this age.

You will, however, see some of their behaviors mirrored during early adolescence. In many ways, these two periods of development are alike because at each stage children are developing autonomy and independence. You may see the same tantrum-like behavior, except that it is more pronounced and sophisticated in the 11- to 14-year-old. At both stages, there are major changes in physical, intellectual, self-, social, and emotional development.

To continue the tricycle to bicycle example, parents of preschoolers need to help their children learn to "ride without training wheels." In other words, as children grow, parents must gradually let go, allowing children to explore their surroundings and learn to enjoy the freedom of their expanding world. Because many new experiences lie ahead, wise parents know that they need to encourage the autonomy and independence characteristic of the preschool stage of development.

In conclusion, Meyerhoff and White (1986, p. 44) offer the following specific recommendations for parents of preschoolers:

1. Encourage children to explore and investigate the world around them.

2. Provide support and attention as needed. Remember preschoolers have their own philosophy of "I'll do it myself!"

3. Set reasonable limits and do not allow children's unacceptable behavior to continue.

4. Talk to your children often, using words they can understand. Listen attentively to their concerns.

5. Encourage children's pretend activities, especially those in which they act out adult roles.

6. Try not to win all arguments, especially during the second half of the second year, when children go through a natural period of negativism.

7. Try not to spoil your children, giving them the notion that the world was made just for them.

4

■■■■■■■■■■■■■■■■■■■■■■■■■■■■■■

Middle Childhood

When someone asks you about your childhood, you may auto-matically think about your elementary school years because you have more memories of that period than you do of preschool. And what do you recall? Your memories may include starting school; joining clubs; best friends; favorite (or least favorite) teachers; school performances; overnights or slumber parties; being (or not being) selected for a team during physical education or recess; playing with cars, trucks, dolls, or action figures; and engaging in make-believe play, such as school, house, or doctor. Some devel-opmental theorists have called middle childhood the "best years" of life.

Unfortunately, some of you may also have negative memories of family conflict—abuse, alcoholism, violence, or divorce. These negative experiences no doubt influenced the degree to which you were able to proceed with the normal developmental tasks characteristic of this stage. Regardless of your experience, these are years in which developmental changes continue to have a significant impact.

If you ask children at this age to describe what their lives are like, they will probably make lots of references to friends, school, and play. This is their world. At this point, they are interested in what has an immediate impact on them. Because they are learning and experiencing so much for the first time, these years serve as building blocks for the years to come.

CHARACTERISTICS OF MIDDLE CHILDHOOD

At every stage of development, there are significant memories and lots of first-time experiences. In the middle years, ages 6 through 11, many of these memories and experiences concern starting school and learning to master tasks associated with formal learning. For this reason, this period of development has been called the school years, or the age of *concrete operational thought*, a term that reflects the way children at this age process information.

Because this is a time of relatively slow, steady growth, most parents generally feel this period is more tranquil than the preschool or early adolescent years. Still, in middle childhood children do have numerous "firsts" that can result in anxiety or adjustment. For example, your child may feel nervous about starting first grade, worrying about whether he or she will be able to read, spell, or please the teacher. Maybe your child will enjoy spending more time with friends but be a little afraid of the first overnight away from home. Or perhaps he or she will feel left out if not invited to a birthday party or selected for the kickball team.

Parents have some adjustments to make as well. Children gradually become less dependent. They begin associating more with their friends and spending more time away from home. In addition, parents may be anxious about their children's learning: Will my child achieve in school? Should I help with homework? Will he or she get along well with teachers and peers?

As is the case for the other stages, you'll see changes in your child's physical, intellectual, self-, social, and emotional development. In the following pages, these changes are discussed; examples of typical problems and ways to address them are also described.

PHYSICAL DEVELOPMENT

Your 6-year-old child wiggles his loose tooth, working it around with his tongue in order to loosen it more quickly. He is excited to lose it because he wants to put it under his pillow and have the Tooth Fairy leave him some money!

Children keep the Tooth Fairy busy for the next 6 years. At about age 6, they lose the bottom front teeth, and by age 12, the last of the baby teeth fall out. School pictures during this period are interesting . . . the toothless smiles gradually disappear, only to be replaced by permanent teeth that seem far too big. Losing teeth is only one of the physical changes that occur in the elementary school years. Although there is no rapid growth spurt, as in adolescence, gradual significant changes in height, weight, and strength do take place.

The average 6-year-old child stands about 3½ feet tall and weighs approximately 45 pounds. During this period, expect your child to get taller and heavier, gaining an average of 2 to 3 inches and approximately 5 to 7 pounds a year. The increase of weight is largely due to increases in the size of the skeletal and muscular systems, as well as the size of other body organs. There is also a gradual decrease in the growth of fatty tissue and an increase in bone and muscle. You will notice that boys develop muscles more rapidly than girls, while girls tend to retain thicker layers of fat. The fatty tissue is distributed so that a girl has rounder, smoother, and softer contours.

You will also notice that the growth spurt in height and weight at the end of this period of development occurs about 2 years earlier for girls than for boys. The physical differences between the sexes and even among members of the same sex may cause embarrassment. Children need sensitivity and support because they may feel self-conscious about being taller, shorter, fatter, or thinner than their peers. It may help to point out to them that everyone comes in a different shape and size—and that most differences will even out as they mature.

Depending on the rate of maturity, some 10- and 11-year-olds may enter puberty. Some girls could begin to develop breasts and start their periods. These changes may also cause a feeling of being different. Parents need to be alert to this and openly discuss these bodily changes with children.

During this period, children's muscular control continues to develop. Their control of large muscles is considerably better than their control of smaller muscles. This explains why children's printing in first and second grades is big and uneven. By the end of the elementary school years, however, children's control of their large muscles is almost perfect, and their control of their small muscles is much improved.

Changes also occur in children's locomotor skills, agility, coordination, and physical strength that make it possible for them to engage in more sophisticated forms of play and sports. For example, they become more competent at running, throwing, climbing, catching, swimming, jumping rope, bike riding, and skating. These physical skills are a source of pleasure and mastery.

CHAPTER 4

Whether we like it or not, as children develop physically there are gender-related differences in motor skills. According to Butterfield and Loovis (1993), differences in motor activity between boys and girls appear as early as the preschool years. These gender differences become even more pronounced in elementary school. Boys show slightly more advanced abilities in areas requiring force and power, such as jumping and running. They can throw with more force and power than girls, and they get better at batting, dribbling, and catching. Girls demonstrate more advanced fine motor skills, such as drawing and penmanship. Their advanced physical maturity enables them to perform better in activities requiring balance and precision, such as hopping and skipping.

Parents need to keep in mind that these gender differences are influenced by parental messages and cultural stereotypes. If parents buy footballs for boys and jump ropes for girls or hold higher expectations for athletic performance for boys than for girls, children will begin to behave in ways that meet these expectations. It is crucial for parents to be conscious of the messages they send to their sons and daughters in this regard.

As children develop physically, the good news is that, generally, they experience fewer illnesses than in the preschool years. Exercise, good nutrition, and the right amount of sleep can help children stay physically fit and healthy.

A Typical Physical Development Problem: Eating Habits and Weight

A couple has been trying their best to get their son to stop eating so much, especially junk food. They are worried that he will gain more weight. Already, at age 8, he weighs 95 pounds but is only 4 feet 2 inches tall. He does not like to exercise, instead preferring to sit in front of the television and snack on chips and soda.

His parents have tried a number of approaches to deal with this problem—reducing meal portions, limiting television time, and scheduling walks and exercise times. Their measures seem to work for a few days, and then their son goes back to his old routine.

The problem with overweight children is a growing one, especially in this country. According to Seifert and Hoffnung (1993), some 80% of children who are overweight remain so as adults. Several things cause obesity and overweight:

Heredity (fat children tend to have fat parents)

Lack of knowledge about healthy diet

Family dysfunction, which creates stress that children then try to alleviate by eating

Use of food as a reward, whereby the child begins to associate food with warmth, comfort, and relief of tension

Maladaptive eating habits, such as eating too fast and not chewing food thoroughly

Lack of physical activity, which in some obese children is also associated with excessive television viewing

Eating high-fat, high-calorie foods, such as soft drinks, sweets, and chips

Family modeling of unhealthy eating habits

Obese and overweight children suffer emotionally, socially, and physically. The physical consequences include high blood pressure and cholesterol levels, along with respiratory abnormalities. These symptoms are strong predictors of heart disease and early death. Emotional consequences include feelings of low self-esteem, depression, and behavior problems. Obese and overweight children suffer from peer rejection, teasing, and ridicule, all of which lead to more negative evaluations of self, aggressive behavior, and loneliness.

What can you do if your child is obese or overweight?

1. It is best to do something about overeating or obesity problems in childhood, before harmful behaviors become well established. A family-based approach is worth considering. In this approach, both the parents and child alter their eating patterns. This may mean eating less fat and fewer sweets, eliminating junk foods, and cutting out fast foods.

2. Encourage exercise, active play, or team sports. Family time could also be devoted to activities like bike riding or roller skating.

3. Curtail television watching because it robs the child of more active playtime. (Children also tend to snack as they watch television.)

4. Consider a chart to monitor daily exercise and healthy eating. You could try establishing an incentive system whereby family members earn points for exercising, eating healthy snacks, and eating nutritious meals every day. The points could be used toward special family activities.

5. Teach your child about healthy eating by helping him or her identify "stop," "go," and "caution" foods. The child can cut out pictures from magazines to represent the various types "Stop" foods include candy, cookies, potato chips, french fries, and the like. "Go" foods include fruits, vegetables, nonsweetened cereals, and lean meats. "Caution" foods are those that should be eaten in moderation—for example, nondiet sodas, cheese, or crackers. The knowledge gained from this activity can help the child make good choices and take ultimate control of his or her own weight, thus avoiding a power struggle with parents.

INTELLECTUAL DEVELOPMENT

Can you remember what you were like when you first started school? Were you among those who asked more questions than adults around you could answer? If so, were you interested in simple, truthful answers instead of long lectures? Can you also remember delighting in telling and listening to jokes and riddles and using your imagination?

In all likelihood, you were very anxious for school to start so you could master reading, writing, and math skills. As you moved from grade to grade in elementary school, you probably noticed changes in your thinking. It became more logical, and you started to realize the importance of rules and regulations. According to the psychologist Robert Havighurst (1972), you were involved in the process of achieving the main developmental task of this period—developing ideas, conscience, morality, and a set of values necessary for everyday living.

To understand the development of thinking in school-age children, we return to the ideas of Jean Piaget. Piaget (1950) described the school years as the period when *concrete operational thought* emerges. That means children become able to process information in a systematic, logical manner when it is presented in a concrete form. For example, it is easier for children at this stage to understand how to tell time if you show them a clock. If you are trying to teach them how to tie their shoes, they learn more quickly if you demonstrate the process and then help them do it. Because they are concrete thinkers, they tend to interpret things literally and misinterpret things because they see them in an either-or way. For example, if a friend doesn't sit by a child, the child may think it is because the two aren't friends anymore.

Because the child can't think more abstractly or consider other possibilities, his or her perception of the event is limited.

Children are also beginning to take into account several aspects of a situation when solving problems. For example, when they are presented with two identical balls of clay and asked if the balls are the same size, they usually agree that they are. If the shape of one ball of clay is changed so that it is flat rather than round, at the time during this stage when children become concrete operational thinkers, they will tell you that the amount of clay is still the same. To solve this problem, they consider both the shape of the clay and whether something was taken away from or added to it. In other words, children now are not easily misled by appearances when solving problems of this nature.

The example just presented describes one of the changes that distinguish the nature of thinking at this stage. Another change in thinking that allows children to solve this problem is *reversible thought*, or the ability to imagine the process whereby something returns to its original state. Children looking at the flattened clay can picture rolling it back into its original round shape so it looks like the other clay ball again. Reversible thought allows children to understand that many actions can be undone by use of an opposite, or reverse, action.

Another aspect of thought that you might observe among school-age children is *transformational thought*. Children demonstrate this type of thinking by paying attention to the process of transformation in an action. In the ball-of-clay example, children will now pay attention to what the ball looks like before its shape changes and notice the transformation in shape as the clay is flattened. In other words, they think about the problem at hand by reconstructing past events before deciding on an answer.

Children at this age are also able to make inferences when they attempt to solve problems. They do this by attending to all the relevant factors related to the situation. Children are able to infer that because nothing was added to or subtracted from the flattened ball of clay, it must have the same amount of clay as the round one.

In addition, school-age children will be able to sort objects into groups according to some common property, such as color, size, or shape. They will also be able to put a series of objects in order according to some relationship, such as arranging sticks from shortest to longest. You will notice that both of these abilities are possible as long as the objects are concrete, not imaginary or abstract.

As a result of the various changes in children's thought processes, they can count many objects and assign each its proper number without skipping any item or counting any item twice. They are also able to solve more challenging problems and use strategies for remembering—saying things out loud to themselves; grouping things by categories instead of trying to remember individual items; and using mnemonics, such as "Every Good Boy Does Fine" to remember the lines on a musical staff.

Children at this age display a number of other changes in their intellectual development. There is a notable change in their morals from using strategies to avoid punishment to using strategies to maximize pleasure. Now children follow the maxim "If it feels good, do it!" Because they assume that adults define what is right and wrong, it is very common to hear children protesting, "It's not fair!" They tend to base their moral decisions on their own needs and desires.

As they begin to venture out and explore their environment, children this age develop a sense of competence and importance. It's a big day for them when they are allowed to ride their bikes to the grocery store all by themselves, and when they can do it without getting lost, they feel skillful and proud.

Furthermore, the egocentric and magical view of the world characteristic of the preschool age is being replaced by a more objective, realistic outlook. Children no longer think everything is possible. Instead, they gather and organize facts and build logical expectations. For example, after reading a storybook, you might hear a third grader exclaiming, "This story is not true. How could that be?" This may also be the age when children worry that Santa Claus won't be able to come down the chimney because there is a fire in the fireplace. Although they begin to question the reality of things, it is important to remember that this change takes place gradually. Children don't lose the imaginative powers they had in preschool. On the contrary, they continue to be imaginative and engage in lots of make-believe play at least through second or third grade.

In contrast to preschoolers, whose sense of time is very immediate, school-age children have a more mature perception of time. For example, if you inform a second grader that her grandparents are coming to visit next week, she won't sit by the window and wait for their car to pull in the driveway, as a preschooler might do. As children get older, they develop a clear understanding of how to tell time and of the concept of minutes, hours, days, and weeks. Despite this ability, they still find it difficult to project very far into the future. Consequently, informing them of plans too far in advance won't be meaningful.

Finally, it helps parents to bear in mind that despite the major changes that take place, children at this age are still guided more by feelings than by reason. For example, they make up facts on the spot to prove that their opinion is right. They also fail to integrate their experiences and do not see complex connections between and among things, such as in the different clues to solving a mystery. Seeing things in an either-or fashion—as good or bad, right or wrong—makes it hard for them to consider possibilities.

A Typical Intellectual Development Problem: Taking Things Too Literally

"My teacher never calls on me to be the helper. He's always telling me to be quiet when other kids talk, too. How come he doesn't like me?" Does this sound like something your third grader might say? What about a fourth grader who gets his math test back with a low grade and assumes that his teacher will think he's stupid or tell him he has to stay in fourth grade and take math again? What about the fifth grader who is upset because she thinks no one likes her? When you ask her more about this, you learn that she thinks this is because her two best friends didn't sit by her in lunch yesterday or play with her during free time.

These examples have two things in common: First, they reflect the concern for approval and acceptance by teachers and peers. Second, they show how literally school-age children take things. Because they still think so concretely and see things in terms of either-or, they readily make assumptions and overgeneralize about issues.

If your child thinks too literally, what can you do?

1. Help your child look at the facts instead of making assumptions (guessing about the situation). Play a game where you each tell something you see about each other, then tell something you guess or assume about each other. For example: "I see that you have on a red T-shirt. I assume red is your favorite color." After doing this several times, discuss the fact that assumptions can be wrong unless they are checked out. Discuss how facts and assumptions apply to the child's situation with teacher, friends, or parents.

2. Help the child look at his or her "track record." It is natural for third and fourth graders to be more concerned about their intellectual activities because they are more aware of how they compare to others. However, you can encourage your child to see that

he or she has done things well in the past. Write these accomplishments down so the child can see, in a concrete way, how successes and failures balance out.

3. Use a continuum (a line drawn on a sheet of paper or a strip of masking tape on the floor) to teach the child how to put situations in perspective. One end of the line is "always," and one end is "never." If your child is feeling rejected by a friend, for example, you can ask the child to put a mark on the line to represent how many times in the last week a friend sat by him or her. Doing this can help the child see the reality of the situation.

SELF-DEVELOPMENT

What responses are you likely to get if you ask 11-year-old children to tell you about themselves? Most likely, they will give you a list of concrete, observable characteristics, such as their name, sex, and something about their appearance. Equally likely, they will refer to a set of psychological traits, such as being helpful, honest, moody, or cheerful. In other words, they will describe their personalities to you.

The many cognitive changes that occur in children's intellectual development, coupled with their expanding social world, contribute greatly to their personality development. In this section, we will describe various aspects of children's developing personalities—how they perceive themselves, how socially competent they feel, their thoughts about sex roles, and their standards of right and wrong.

As children enter school, they encounter a series of new tasks. If they complete these tasks successfully, they develop a sense of mastery and achievement. If they fail repeatedly, they develop feelings of inadequacy and incompetence. Children learn to win the recognition of parents, peers, teachers, and other adults by producing things. The recognition they receive from others—in the form of praise, for example—helps them see that others consider them worthwhile and competent. On the baseball diamond, they practice to demonstrate their playing skills. In the classroom, they practice their math, reading, and writing skills. If children do not receive positive remarks from adults about their skills and performance, they gradually give up and develop a sense of inadequacy that makes it difficult for them to try again.

Closely related to the development of a sense of achievement is children's ability to perceive themselves and understand how others perceive them. Children begin to understand the impact of their behaviors on others. This awareness encourages them to monitor their actions. Thus, they act differently depending on whom they are with. As they get older, they become more self-conscious and cautious regarding how much of themselves they wish to reveal to others.

As they begin to compare themselves to others, they make judgments about their appearance, abilities, and behavior in relation to other children. They incorporate this information into their self-concept. As children move into adolescence, their sources for self-definition become more selective. The feedback they receive from their close friends becomes most important to them.

Children's awareness of themselves also grows during this period. Some evaluate themselves positively, while others evaluate themselves negatively. Obviously, children who make positive judgments about their worth or goodness feel good about themselves and evaluate their skills highly. Parents seem to have a high degree of influence over their children's positive self-esteem. According to results of interviews conducted by Coopersmith (1967), parents of children with high self-esteem were described as being affectionate, helpful, available, fair, competent, concerned, and promoters of individual freedom.

However, children's self-esteem actually declines in the first few years of elementary school. Parents, do not be alarmed! The drop in self-esteem from the preschool period is generally not enough to be detrimental and occurs because children gradually adjust their self-judgments to fit the opinions of others as they enter school. It is important for parents to try to help children evaluate their performance objectively and realistically in order to preserve their self-acceptance and self-respect.

A Typical Self-Development Problem:
Feeling Incompetent

It is the tenth week of school. Your fourth-grade daughter's teacher calls to share concern about your daughter's performance in class. The teacher explains that your child rarely volunteers to answer questions, doesn't participate in classroom discussions, and is almost an unnoticeable presence in the classroom. When the teacher calls on your daughter, she gets nervous and falters in her answers. In a one-to-one conversation with the teacher, your daughter has said, "I just can't do anything right! I'm dumb. When I try, I just fail. So why should I try again?"

These cries of incompetence and failure are common among some school age children, and many parents have to deal with problems such as this one. As a parent, you play a major role in helping your child develop confidence in his or her ability. The following suggestions may be useful.

1. If your child doesn't perform particularly well in school, engage him or her in hobbies to develop mastery and a sense of achievement in something other than schoolwork. Help him or her see how to succeed in order to help build academic confidence.

2. Encourage your child to join organizations such as Boy Scouts or Girl Scouts and other community organizations. Participation in these types of groups also helps develop skills and interests in areas apart from schoolwork.

3. Help your child see that he or she is not like a balloon: If the child doesn't perform well in math, for example, that doesn't mean he or she deflates to nothing. Instead, explain that the child's abilities are more like the spokes on a wheel: There are lots of them, some stronger than others. Not every spoke needs to be perfect for the wheel to do its job.

4. When you see your child doing something well or improving at something, comment on it: "I think you really studied hard for that test. It shows me that you care about your work." This takes the focus off the end product—in this case, the grade.

5. Encourage effort and perseverance by reading stories such as *The Little Engine That Could* by Piper (1961) for younger children and *Knots on a Counting Rope* by Martin (1987) for older children. Children need to understand that succeeding at something takes effort.

SOCIAL DEVELOPMENT

The social world of school-age children expands beyond the family to include peers and teachers, from whom children continue to learn about the values, behaviors, and beliefs that will enable them to become functioning members of society. In this section, we discuss four major aspects of social development in school-age children: sex-role development, peer relations, relations with parents, and school influences.

An 8-year-old boy touched a girl. The girl squealed, "Boy's germs, boy's germs!" A 9-year-old girl was reading a list of people coming to a birthday party. When her father asked whether boys were invited, she replied emphatically, "No boys are invited!" When a 10-year-old boy was asked if he wanted to play with a same-age neighbor girl, he replied by saying, "I don't play with sissy girls!"

These incidents illustrate the fact that school-age children tend to relate to and play almost exclusively with children of their own sex. For example, at recess girls play on one side of the playground, boys on the other; girls invite only girls and boys invite only boys to birthday parties. Sex segregation is usually most pronounced in the third grade.

Cultural stereotypes of masculine and feminine roles explain why boys and girls hold such rigid views. School-age children associate being tough, aggressive, and dominant with masculinity and being gentle, excitable, and affectionate with femininity. These stereotypes contribute significantly to the different interests and activities of boys and girls. Despite changing sex roles, media, peers, and parents play a major role in perpetuating stereotypes.

It is important for parents to remember that during the elementary school years their children extend their sex-stereotyped beliefs to personality and achievement. Parents can expect their boys' sex-role identities to strengthen and their daughters' to become more flexible. That is, boys will stick rigidly to their "masculine" activities, whereas girls will engage in more traditionally male activities, such as organized sports.

Another important aspect of social development for parents to anticipate is the steady increase in peer interactions. Don't be surprised if by fourth, fifth, and sixth grade your child wants to spend most of his or her time with friends. This is an important part of development; by spending time outside the family, children develop a broader view of the world, experiment with ideas, and learn social interaction skills that prepare them for the future. As they participate in activities, they learn to cooperate and compromise, make and break rules, take roles as leaders and followers, and understand their peers' points of view. Clubs, camps, and organized groups such as 4-H or scouts are important places to further develop these social skills.

Being popular and accepted by peers is a significant concern for school-age children. In the early grades, children may be accepted into a peer group if they have certain noticeable characteristics, such as pretty hair or a nice-sounding name. In later grades, children's criteria for acceptance changes to emphasize personal qualities such as honesty, kindness, or humor.

Most, if not all, children like to be popular. But once popular, a child does not necessarily continue to be popular. A child or group popular one year may not be the following year. In general, though, popular children tend to be good at initiating and maintaining social interactions and understanding social situations. They know that acceptance into a group is a gradual process that takes work. Peers rate popular children as being confident, good-natured, and athletic. They are well liked and sought after as friends. Unpopular children, on the other hand, are rated by their peers as being unpleasant, disruptive, aggressive, and selfish. They are not included in activities, and their peers don't seek them out as friends.

Peer relationships can be negative as well as positive for several reasons. First, in the upper grades, children begin to exclude others and can be cruel with teasing. Second, there may be negative peer pressures to engage in inappropriate activities. In addition, an unhealthy sense of competition can sometimes develop in peer groups.

Although peers become increasingly important during this period, parents continue to be a strong influence on their school-age children. Children begin to learn more about their parents' attitudes and why their parents make family rules. That makes children more able to control their behavior, thereby improving the relationship with their parents. Children do not need to be monitored as closely as they did in earlier years. Instead, parents need to monitor their children indirectly to encourage them to take care of themselves and develop responsibility and independence.

Next to parents, teachers are the most powerful and influential adults in the life of school-age children. From teachers, children learn many social behaviors and develop attitudes toward authority, school, and society. The ideal teacher is supportive, nurturing, and enthusiastic. He or she can have a significant impact on the child's self-esteem.

A Typical Social Development Problem: Dealing with Teasing and Put-downs

"You bat the ball like an idiot."

"Your hair sucks!"

"You laugh like a hyena."

"You won't make the team because you run like a turtle."

Unfortunately, remarks like these are common among school-age children. Depending on a child's self-esteem, these words can be like bullets, penetrating and stirring up negative feelings. Although most children experience anger, hurt, or sadness when they are the victims of this type of teasing, the most vulnerable are those who take these words to heart and begin to withdraw from peers because they can't tolerate the teasing. Although no one likes to be teased or put down, it is very difficult to control what other children say. Therefore, it is important to help your child learn some ways to tolerate teasing.

If your child complains about being teased or put down, what can you do?

1. Teach the child rhymes, jingles, or songs, such as "Sticks and stones can break my bones, but words can never hurt me." Discuss the idea that the child doesn't have to believe what others say or let the words hurt.

2. Help the child develop a defense against teasing. You might suggest that the child use his or her imagination to build a wall to block out the teasing words.

3. Teach your child to ask, "Am I what they say I am?" For example, if someone calls the child a pig, have the child look in a mirror and ask, "Do I look like a pig?" When the answer is no, tell the child that if the teasing isn't true, he or she can choose not to be upset by it.

4. If none of these things works, remember that sometimes a group of children can be unreasonably cruel. In this case, contact the school or the parents to help resolve the problem.

EMOTIONAL DEVELOPMENT

Your 10-year-old son is feeling very guilty. Instead of putting his laundry in the dresser as he was asked to do, he shoved it underneath his bed so you would not find it. When you asked if he was finished putting his clothes away, he said he had. Although you did not find out what he did, your son lay in bed, feeling bad because he had lied. Despite the fact that you were not monitoring his behavior, he still realized he did something wrong.

This example indicates the way children of school age begin to experience more complex emotions, such as guilt, shame, or pride. Children at this age are also increasingly aware that people are capable of experiencing more than one emotion at a time. For example, an 8-year-old child said to her mother, "I am happy I went to the movie with you, but unhappy because I didn't like it." Furthermore, they become more adept at hiding their own emotions when it is socially appropriate to do so. For instance, your son may tell a friend he had a good time at the friend's party but tell you he was bored.

School-age children also become better able to control their emotions by devising ways to handle negative emotional situations. For example, they learn to feel less upset about a bad grade by distracting themselves by reading a book, watching television, or playing with friends. Older school-age children may use positive reminders to deal with such situations, saying, for example, "Things could be worse. I'll do better on other tests."

In addition to recognizing and responding to their own feelings, school-age children become more aware of others' thoughts and feelings. They discover consistent patterns of behavior in the people they know, and they may begin to describe them in terms of psychological traits—honest, humorous, moody, and so forth. Such descriptions enable children to recognize that others may react to social situations or interpret the same event quite differently from the way they do. Their awareness that other people may have thoughts and feelings different from their own allows them to respond to other people's needs more effectively. According to Eisenberg (1987), children who can imagine what other people may be thinking and feeling are able to display empathy and sympathy, handle difficult social situations, and resolve everyday misunderstandings. On the other hand, children who have difficulty imagining the thoughts and feelings of others tend to mistreat adults and peers without feeling guilty for their actions.

The final issue related to school-age children's emotional development concerns fears or worries. You will recall that preschoolers' fears resulted from their inability to distinguish between reality and fantasy. Although this inability may continue into first or second grade (depending on how soon children develop concrete thinking skills), children's fears ultimately become more specific and realistic. They may be afraid of physical danger or bodily harm, bad storms or accidents, or being left home alone. They also worry about a variety of other issues—friends, grades, sickness, or whether or not they will be chosen for a team.

In addition to specific fears, school-age children might experience school phobia. Has your child ever complained about having a stomachache, a headache, an earache, or a sore throat just before breakfast on a school day? Has your child seemed to feel better after you allowed him or her to stay home? If you answered yes, your child was likely experiencing school phobia. Fear of school is common among both boys and girls in the early elementary years as they go through the transition to a new setting. They express their phobia either by making excuses in order not to go to school or by becoming intensely anxious while there.

School-age children seem to exhibit two forms of school phobia. The first form appears during the first or second grade. The child prefers to stay home instead of going to school, perhaps because of feelings of anxiety about leaving the parents. Parents can deal with this first form by standing firm and not giving in to the child's excuses to stay home. The sooner parents do this, the less likely it is that a pattern of staying home will be established. The second form of school phobia is more typical of older students who have experienced some difficulties or unpleasant experiences in school or at home. To deal with this second form, parents need to explore the sources of the difficulties in the child's life and seek professional help if the situation continues.

A Typical Emotional Development Problem: Anxiety

The parents of one 8-year-old girl are puzzled by their daughter's anxiety about bad things happening to her family and by her constant worry about being hurt in a car accident or in a storm. The parents recall their daughter's seeing a car accident while they were driving, but it was minor one, and no one was injured. They also remember their daughter's experience at her grandmother's house, when a tornado touched down nearby. During this event, the girl and her grandmother sought shelter in the storm cellar, where they were trapped for a short while because they were not strong enough to push the door open. The parents know that their daughter is generally well adjusted, has many friends, does well in school, and presents no problem at home except typical sibling conflict. However, they are concerned about her anxiety.

If your child shows similar worries and anxieties, what should you do?

1. Take your child's worries seriously, but remember that it is not uncommon for children this age to overgeneralize about situations and imagine the worst.

2. Teach your child positive self-talk to reinforce the idea that, although bad things can happen, it is not

necessary to worry every day. Examples of positive self-talk may be "Just because there is a bad storm does not mean there will be a tornado" or "My parents are old, and they've never been in a car accident. If they drive carefully, they probably won't be in an accident."

3. Empower the child by taking more safety precautions, such as installing additional smoke alarms and fire extinguishers in your house and teaching specific safety tips to follow during fires, storms, and the like.

4. Teach the child how to put problems in perspective. If your child is afraid of storms, you could make a chart showing all different types of weather—sun, clouds, rain, wind, thunderstorms, tornadoes. Watch the weather report with your child and have him or her chart the weather each day for a week or two. Because this is a concrete activity, it will help the child see that the event is not a common occurrence.

CONCLUSION

Imagine that you are watching home movies of your elementary-age child. Even though the developmentalists maintain that this is a period of gradual development, it may not seem that way to you as you watch the years unfold. It may seem like yesterday when your little first grader strapped on a backpack, grinned a toothless smile, and tripped off to school. Suddenly, you had a second grader who was reading everything in sight. Soon after, it seemed, you were taking your fourth grader to camp. As you found yourself explaining puberty to your 11-year-old, you realized how many changes actually occurred during the past 6 years.

As you prepare for early adolescence, step back and appreciate the many changes represented in the years of middle childhood:

Learning the academic "firsts"—reading, writing, spelling, adding and subtracting, and telling time

Learning to socialize—to cooperate, compete, and compromise

Expressing more complex emotions and communicating thoughts and feelings more effectively

Thinking and reasoning more logically

As children progress from the inquisitive "whats and whys" of first grade to the challenging "whats and whys" that begin to emerge at the end of sixth grade, remember that their thinking is slowly becoming more abstract. As their bodies develop, so do their minds. What they have achieved during the middle childhood years is the foundation for early adolescence.

5

Early Adolescence

Close your eyes and think about being 13 or 14 years old. What do you remember—talking on the phone to your friends, spending hours alone in your room with the stereo blasting, or scrutinizing your changing body, feature by feature? Some of you will no doubt remember that arguments with parents were more frequent— arguments about your whereabouts, your friends, your grades, or your habits. If you were to do a survey, you would probably learn that most parents would not want to be this age again because many of them remember more turbulence associated with this period of development than with childhood and mid-adolescence.

Because early adolescence can be a challenging period, both for teenagers and their parents, we decided to ask several 13- and 14-year-olds what advice they would like to give to parents. Here are their responses:

> "Don't stand and argue with me if we're having a fight. Give me space to calm down."

> "If you tell me something and I get the point, don't keep telling me a hundred times."

> "Don't treat me like I'm stupid. Just because I'm a kid doesn't mean I'm dumb."

97

"Don't keep bringing up all the bad things I do. Don't blow it all out of proportion and think that I'll never change."

"If I ask you something and you tell me no, and I ask why, don't say that you don't have to give me a reason. Treat me like an adult."

"Don't tell me that I should be like my older sister. It makes me feel bad and 'second best,' like I'm not good enough for you."

"Appreciate me for what I do and try to understand me and my feelings."

"Don't assume that I'll do bad things or screw up."

As you read this list, you probably remember doing some of the things these teenagers advise against. Such behaviors and attitudes may be natural, but they don't encourage good parent-adolescent relationships. You may be thinking that your teenager wants you to be instantly transformed into an accepting, compliant parent who never raises his or her voice, sets limits, or makes requests. That scenario doesn't feel right either. Furthermore, it isn't the best way to parent. However, because young adolescents are struggling to maintain some sort of equilibrium between their emotional ups and downs and to establish themselves as independent individuals, you will need to reevaluate your parenting practices to relate more effectively to your child at this stage of development.

CHARACTERISTICS OF EARLY ADOLESCENCE

Early adolescence begins at about age 11 for girls and lasts until about age 14. It begins somewhat later and lasts somewhat longer for boys. It is important to remember that, aside from the period from birth to age 2, more changes occur during early adolescence than at any other stage of development. As a result, it may seem to you that one night you tell your 12-year-old goodnight and the next morning you wake up to a complete stranger! As one father stated, "Yesterday my son was building castles with blocks, and today he stood for hours in front of the mirror, agonizing over a pimple and a misplaced hair."

Keep in mind that some children enter this stage later than others, so if your 13-year-old isn't becoming more private, isn't obsessed with his or her looks, or isn't constantly on the phone with friends, don't count your blessings yet! In all likelihood, all these things will occur, although some will naturally depend on the individual personality of the child. Also, rest assured that a complete personality change doesn't occur during adolescence. If your 8-year-old was well adjusted, did well in school, was essentially a happy child, and generally got along well with you, this basic pattern isn't going to undergo a complete metamorphosis. Granted, there will be some changes during this period of rapid emotional, physical, and intellectual growth. However, the intensity and rate of problems associated with this period depend on a number of variables, including your child's basic personality structure and your ability to disregard the stereotype that the "terrible teens" are worse than the "terrible twos."

According to Douglas Schave and Barbara Schave (1989), what the young adolescent experiences is part of a normal, healthy developmental process. They contend that most teenagers negotiate this phase without extreme difficulty. This does not necessarily imply smooth sailing, although it is important to note that the majority of adolescents do not resort to drug dependence, delinquent acting out, school failure, sexual promiscuity, or other self-destructive behaviors. Many researchers maintain that the horror stories we hear about adolescence are simply not true despite the fact that these myths are passed on from generation to generation.

Laurence Steinberg and Ann Levine (1987) agree with Schave and Schave's position that some adolescents are troubled and do get into problems, but they emphasize that those youths are probably the ones who had problems when they were younger. They express concern that many of the problems society may see as part of "normal" adolescence—drugs, delinquency, oppositional behavior, and irresponsible sex—are not at all normal. They believe so much attention has been placed on delinquents, dropouts, and pregnant teens that we have neglected to look at ordinary adolescents.

And who is the "ordinary" adolescent? It is probably your son or daughter, who is trying to achieve more independence in a variety of ways, who has more need for emotional and physical privacy, who doesn't want to be seen with you because he or she doesn't want to appear "babyish," and who chooses friends over family. Because of the numerous hormonal, physical, and social changes during this period of development, the "ordinary" adolescent goes through varying degrees of emotional upheaval that can result in defensive, temperamental, or ultrasensitive behavior. It is very easy for parents to mistake this behavior for defiance and to overreact, which in turn results in conflict. Perhaps the best advice is to keep a level head. Remember that the outbursts aren't about *you*; they are usually just the natural consequence of the hormonal eruption. Those behaviors are often as frustrating to adolescents as to parents. More specific guidelines for dealing with these behaviors are offered later in the chapter.

The following descriptions of the young adolescent's physical, intellectual, self-, social, and emotional development should help you understand more about what your adolescent is experiencing and what you can expect during this period. Following each description is an example of a typical problem, along with specific suggestions for handling the concern.

Physical Development

During early adolescence, physical changes occur more rapidly than at any other period of development except infancy. The essence of puberty is captured by Anne Frank (1963), in *The Diary of a Young Girl*:

> Yesterday I read an article . . . it might have been addressed to me personally . . . about a girl in the years of puberty who becomes quiet within and begins to think about the wonders that are happening to her body. I experience that too, and that is why I get the feeling lately of being embarrassed about Margot, Mummy, and Daddy . . . I think what is happening to me is so wonderful, and not only what can be seen on my body, but all that is taking place inside. (p. 115)

Not all adolescents experience these changes with as much enthusiasm as Anne Frank. Because all parts of the body do not grow at the same time or rate, there is a good deal of awkwardness during this period. Furthermore, just when it is so important to fit in and be like their peers, many adolescents are self-conscious because their feet are too big for their bodies, their breasts are too large or too small, or their voices crack at unpredictable times. Teenagers feel like their bodies are out of control. They are embarrassed if they are developing faster or slower than their peers—almost a guarantee because adolescents enter puberty at different ages and because some complete it in 2 years, whereas others need 5 or 6 years to mature.

Because of the extreme variation in the rate of physical maturation, this can be one of the most eventful periods of development. Early maturers are generally more active in school affairs, more socially mature, more self-confident, and more athletic than late maturers. At the same time, females especially are embarrassed by their femininity and are reluctant to discuss their physical changes with peers. Late maturers feel more self-conscious and frustrated by their rate of development. They worry about being teased or disliked. Regardless of whether they mature early or late, all young teens worry to some extent about their physical attractiveness.

At approximately age 11 for females and age 13 for males, a growth spurt begins, with increases in height and weight accompanied by a redistribution of body tissue and change in proportion. This growth spurt lasts approximately 3 years. Because it begins about 2 years earlier for females than for males, it is very common to see the girls towering over the boys at a junior high dance. This growth spurt affects adolescents in several ways. First, it has a major impact on how well they perform certain physical activities. They may be uncoordinated, for example, because their hands or feet are disproportionate to other body parts. Second, their physical development influences the way others perceive them, and they may be embarrassed by others' comments about this. Third, their development affects how they see themselves, and because they are so preoccupied with their rate of development in comparison to others, they may go to extremes to avoid situations where they have to undress in front of peers.

The first sign of puberty for the adolescent female is swelling around the nipples, which can begin any time between the ages of 8 and 13. Full breast development takes several years. Shortly after the breasts begin to develop, pubic hair appears and hips begin to fill out. Underarm hair appears anywhere from age 13 to 16. Menstruation usually begins between the ages of 10 and 16, most commonly about age 13. Menstruation is a developmental milestone because it signifies that the young female will begin to ovulate and can become pregnant, although full fertility is generally not achieved until about a year after menstruation begins.

For adolescent males, the development of the testicles is the first sign of puberty. At approximately age 12, the testicles become larger, the scrotum becomes darker, and pubic hair develops. In the following year, the penis begins to grow, continuing to enlarge for at least 2 years after that. At about age 14, underarm and facial hair appear, and the male's voice starts to "crack." By age 14 or 15, internal sex organs have begun to develop and males are capable of ejaculating. Initially the sperm count is very low, and they are not fully fertile for about a year. Nocturnal emissions are also very common during this period, as are spontaneous erections. Males, more so than females, have problems with oily skin, perspiration, odor, and acne.

Although adolescents may not ask direct questions, they will be curious about sex. They may wonder if all kids their age feel this way, whether they are crazy for thinking about sex, whether they will know how to "do it" when the time comes, and if it is normal to masturbate. Hormones obviously play a role in sexual feelings and contribute to sexual fantasies. Young adolescents need to know that these fantasies are normal and that masturbation is a natural way to feel sexual pleasure. They also need straightforward information about sex—specifically, that unprotected sex can result in pregnancy and sexually transmitted diseases, including AIDS, and that emotional risks are associated with early sexual activity.

Parents need to begin discussions about puberty and sexual activity before these issues arise, at about age 9 or 10. These topics should be discussed informally, rather than all at once with a "big talk." Discussion can often occur spontaneously as something you see or hear triggers the opportunity to initiate a conversation. For example, you may see that one of your daughter's classmates has begun to develop breasts and ask your daughter if she is wondering when this will start to happen to her. Bringing the subject up in this manner makes this important topic less intimidating.

As a parent, you need to feel comfortable answering questions your adolescent may have. Try to be as straightforward and honest as possible, and, above all, don't simply hand your teenager a book to read. Throughout your conversations, ask questions about what your teenager is feeling or thinking, but don't be surprised if the response is a shrug of the shoulders and an "I don't know." Being available keeps the door open for further discussion at a time when your adolescent may be less embarrassed. It is also important to reassure your teenager that there may be some difficult adjustments but that these are natural changes that all teenagers experience.

A Typical Physical Development Problem: Self-Consciousness

The phone rings. It is your adolescent daughter's best friend. As you overhear bits and pieces of the conversation, you sense your daughter's reluctance to commit to a slumber party over the weekend. Normally she would be begging to go, but lately she hasn't even asked, and she sounds very evasive on the phone. When you question her, she just says that she doesn't feel like spending the night and instead asks to go to a movie with another friend. You don't think much of it, but then you begin to notice that she does not want to go to school on certain days. When you look more closely, you discover that the lack of attendance corresponds with physical education days. As you piece the information together, you sense that the school and overnight social avoidance has to do with your daughter's discomfort about undressing in front of peers. What should you do?

1. Gently discuss the issue with your daughter. Share your assumptions with her. Encourage her to talk about her feelings and tell you whether or not specific teasing or an embarrassing incident has triggered her hesitation to undress in public. Don't be surprised if you don't get much response. Be patient and supportive. The fact that you are acknowledging the problem lets her know you are available for further discussion.

2. Be firm about attending school. School avoidance is rather typical at this stage of development because young men and women don't want others to see their bodies. They are afraid that others will make jokes about the size of their breasts or penises, or they simply may be self-conscious and concerned about how they compare to others. This is very natural, but they need to face the situation rather than avoid it. Reassure them that everyone grows at a different rate and that despite the fact that they feel as though no one is as big or little as they are, that is probably not the case. Stress the fact that people come in all different shapes and sizes and point out that how people look physically is only one aspect of who they are.

3. If the school avoidance persists, talk to the physical education instructor about the supervision in the locker room. It could be that cruel remarks are being made, and the teacher may need to address this with the group. Adolescents are hypersensitive at this age, and they certainly do need to learn to control their own behavior and emotions because they can't control others' behavior. However, it is sometimes very helpful for a teacher to make some general comments to discourage teasing and tormenting.

INTELLECTUAL DEVELOPMENT

During adolescence, the shift from concrete to *formal operational thought* occurs. According to many researchers, this is the most dramatic change in thinking that occurs during the life span, resulting in an increased ability to think abstractly and logically. As they stop thinking in either-or terms, adolescents begin to see the uncertainty and ambiguity of things. Instead of categorizing things as good or bad, right or wrong, they will debate an issue because they recognize that some concepts—such as loyalty, honesty, or fairness—can't be quantified and measured.

This major shift is reflected in the fact that young adolescents begin to think in terms of possibilities. For example, it is easier for them to engage in a debate with parents because they can anticipate parents' possible arguments and prepare their "counterattack" in advance. As a parent, you are probably very familiar with this scenario:

Teenager: Can I stay overnight with Jennifer?

Parent: No, you have to get to bed early so that you'll be ready for your gymnastics meet tomorrow.

Teenager: I can go to bed early at Jennifer's. Her parents always make us go to bed early. Besides, I went to bed early last night and got lots of sleep. I can even sleep on the bus if I'm tired.

Parent: No, I don't think it's a good idea.

Teenager: But, Mom . . . you're not being fair.

The ability to think of different possibilities can be frustrating at times because it is hard to know which option to choose. You may see this exemplified when your teenager asks you what he should wear to a ball game. After you have reeled off the possibilities, you are surprised to see him leave the house in the same clothes he had on when he asked you! It's as if he is overwhelmed by the choices and hasn't yet developed a method for deciding.

In addition to thinking in terms of possibilities, young adolescents are also capable of thinking one thing and saying another. Whereas your 7-year-old had difficulty keeping secrets or telling a lie, your adolescent can be quite ingenious at making up stories to cover up something that will meet with your disapproval. Some adolescents can be so convincing that parents have difficulty knowing when they are hearing the truth.

Because adolescents think in terms of possibilities and don't regard things as absolute, they may be better able to deal with exceptions to rules. For example, your daughter may be quick to respond to your refusal to let her date until she is 16 by informing you that this might have been proper when you were young, but times have changed and now everyone dates before age 16. Adolescents are also quite capable of thinking of logical rebuttals. In response to an admonition about drinking, adolescents may very well point out that if parents have a drink before dinner, why shouldn't they? What they have failed to realize is that there is a law against underage drinking. So while the rebuttals may be logical, parents need to realize that sometimes they don't conform with reality.

It is also quite common for adolescents to be able to think logically in some areas but be unable to apply logic across the board. For instance, they can reason well in advanced math class but can't manage their allowance. Parents are sometimes confused about this inconsistency and assume that it is deliberate. However, formal operational thinking is attained in stages. Therefore, it is normal, albeit frustrating, for adolescents to be inconsistent in applying logical thinking.

During this period of development, young adolescents are able to predict the consequences of their actions—they understand that if they come home past their curfew they could be grounded. They are also beginning to speculate about the logical sequence of events. For example, they can understand that the harder they practice a musical instrument, the better their chances of being selected for the honors band. They can also recognize inconsistencies between policies and practice: Just because there are laws against discrimination doesn't mean that they won't be discriminated against.

Because of their increased ability to see possibilities, young adolescents recognize the gap between the real and the ideal. As a result, they tend to be very skeptical about social issues, such as religion and politics, and begin to question aspects of their parents' convictions and practices. In addition, they are often harsh with and critical of adults, especially parents and teachers.

Other noticeable changes in thinking at this stage include the ability to appreciate puns, sarcasm, and irony. For this reason, *Mad Magazine* and *Saturday Night Live* become favorites. Young adolescents are also better at organization, so parents can hope to see improvement in the way assignments, chores, and other responsibilities are prioritized and managed. The ability to think more abstractly also influences social relationships. Young adolescents are better able to appreciate that the way they perceive and react to some people might not be the way their friends react. They can also begin to understand that their friends might not like everything they do. Gradually, they become more accepting of individual differences.

As a parent, be prepared for the fact that your young adolescent will challenge anything and everything and may initiate discussions or arguments just to try out newly acquired thinking skills! Although the sudden challenge to your authority can be disorienting, try to look at the positive side and see this tendency as part of the process of becoming an independent thinker. You don't want your child to blindly accept everything that comes along! You want your daughter to challenge her friends who try to persuade her that smoking marijuana is harmless or your son to defend his position when his friends try to convince him to shoplift. Above all, keep in mind that open discussions and intellectual debates help your teenager develop an inquisitive mind and independent thinking skills. Rather than assuming every argumentative statement is aimed at you personally, recognize that your adolescent is questioning your judgment because he or she is more intellectually mature and is better able to see inconsistencies. That does not mean you should tolerate rudeness or disrespect, but you should expect your adolescent to look for the rationale behind your requests. Because your child is in the process of achieving another milestone in cognitive development, the days of saying "This is the way it is because I'm your parent" and expecting unquestioned compliance are gone.

A Typical Intellectual Development Problem: Challenging Parental Authority

Adolescents are now beginning to think they are the world's foremost authorities on everything. Because they think they know what is best and are more likely at this age to assert themselves by declaring their independence, it is very common to see young adolescents challenging parental authority in a variety of ways. Not coming home on time and thinking they don't need to let parents know where they are rank high on the challenging authority scale. What should you do if your adolescent doesn't come home on time or let you know where he or she is going?

1. First of all, make sure that you have discussed and made clear when the teenager should be home. Next, make sure he or she knows that there will be a consequence for being late. This doesn't mean you should be completely

unreasonable and ground the adolescent if he or she is occasionally 5 or 10 minutes late; however, if lateness becomes a consistent pattern, that is another matter. It is also important to make it clear that you won't buy into the age-old excuses—not knowing what time it is, waiting for a friend, and not being able to find a ride or a phone to call for one. Inform your teenager that you expect him or her to plan ahead to be home on time. If lateness is a chronic problem, apply logical consequences rather than grounding. Teenagers see grounding as punishment. This makes them angry but doesn't necessarily change their behavior. Logical consequences allow adolescents to make their own choices and take responsibility for their own behavior. The consequence should be spelled out in advance and stated calmly— for example, "You can walk over to Theresa's house and spend the afternoon, but you need to be home no later than 4:30. If you aren't, you won't be able to go to the movie with your friends tomorrow night." You could also specify that if your adolescent is 30 minutes late one night, he or she will have to come in 30 minutes earlier the next night. You can inform your teenager in advance that, if late the second night, he or she will not be allowed to go out at night for an entire week since he or she doesn't seem to be able to handle the responsibility. These logical consequences differ from grounding because you have informed your adolescent in advance of them and he or she is the one who chooses to assume control.

2. Be sure not to give in to variations on "But you can't make me stay home next Friday. That's the junior high party." Your response needs to be "I'm really sorry, but you knew what the consequences would be when you made your choice. Maybe next time you'll think it through more carefully." You would be surprised to hear how many teenagers say they know they can get by with things because their parents never follow through. By being consistent, you teach your adolescent responsibility and how to profit from mistakes. If you are inconsistent, you teach that what you say doesn't matter and that your adolescent may as well try to get away with whatever he or she can.

3. Check with the parents of your adolescent's friends. How are they determining when their children should

be home? Some parents establish a standard curfew, while others prefer to determine the time based on the activity. (Doing it the latter way can invite arguing and manipulation, however.) Most adolescents seem to like a curfew because they know in advance what is expected and how much time they have to work with. It is also reasonable to restrict the young adolescent's activities to weekends unless there is a school- or church-sponsored activity during the week.

4. As a parent, you have a right to know where your adolescent is going, what time the event begins and ends, whom he or she will be with, and what the transportation arrangements are. Remember that a teenager's sense of time is much different than yours and that many activities do happen very spontaneously. Therefore, if you ask on Wednesday what is happening on Friday, you will likely hear an exasperated "I have no clue." Don't press it, but do firmly insist that your teen inform you of his or her whereabouts. If you trust your adolescent and approve of his or her friends, it will probably do more harm than good to require a phone call at every single change of activity. However, it is advisable to monitor closely initially and gradually reduce control as your teenager demonstrates honesty and trustworthiness.

SELF-DEVELOPMENT

We could appropriately describe young teenagers as chameleons because they try on so many new ways of thinking, feeling, and behaving in the process of their self-development. In fact, some parents have commented that they are not sure who will come walking down the stairs in the morning—the child who is 12 but who acts 2, or the child who is 12 but who acts 22! In either case, parents need to recognize that this is all part of the process of adjusting to the changes resulting from the teenager's more advanced physical and intellectual development.

The task of self-definition begins during early adolescence. Ironically, as young adolescents strive for self-integration, they may become more dependent on parents. This creates a great deal of ambivalence for them. As a result, they may push for autonomy and at the same time be frightened by it, although they would be the last to admit it! Because they are immature, lack life experiences, and are adjusting to many cognitive, physical, hormonal, and social changes, young adolescents are very vulnerable. In brief, they lack a strong sense of self.

Although it may seem as though they are wasting time, young adolescents are developing a clearer picture of who they are through the hours they spend on the phone, listening to music, and hanging out with friends. Through these interactions, they begin to question values, challenge ideas, and incorporate standards into their concept of self. All of this is critical to forming their own identity, a process that will not be completed until mid-adolescence or later.

In some ways, adolescents contradict themselves. They want people to appreciate their uniqueness, but at the same time, you can't tell them apart. If you were to identify some key phrases to describe them, *selfish, indulgent, self-absorbed,* and *egocentric* may come to mind. It is not unusual for young adolescents to see themselves as more important than they really are or to feel that no one else experiences things the way they do. In many ways, they see themselves as the center of the universe and assume that the world should revolve around them. This does not necessarily imply that they have a good self-concept; many teenagers feel particularly incompetent and physically unattractive during this period. Because they experience a lot of self-doubt, they crave approval. Parents and teachers need to take extra measures to praise effort as well as achievement and to encourage activities and interests in which mastery will result.

It is important not to discount your adolescent's perceptions by giving pep talks or saying that you know he or she is talented, well liked, smart, and so on. If the adolescent doesn't feel positive about himself or herself, your words will fall on deaf ears. Instead, state your opinions as your own: "I understand that you don't think you are smart, but I do" or "I'm proud that you brought your grade up on this last exam. That says to me that you can succeed." To help your teenager break out of an egocentric mind set, structure opportunities for him or her to assume responsibilities that revolve around the family, church, or community.

Feeling unique and egocentric has another negative aspect. Young adolescents may feel that because they are unique, they are invulnerable. David Elkind (1984), a noted authority on child and adolescent development, has labeled this belief the "personal fable." Briefly, because adolescents believe they are special, they also believe bad things can happen to others but not to them. Therefore, they think they can take drugs and not get addicted or be sexually active and not get pregnant. Closely tied to this is the feeling that they are special, famous, or heroic. For this reason, many have unrealistic expectations about what it takes to be truly successful. Parents need to relax and understand that as adolescents mature, their perceptions will change; not too many adolescents actually end up being the famous movie star they aspired to be at the age of 14!

Young adolescents are very self-conscious. They assume that everyone is looking at them and become supersensitive and preoccupied with the response of what Elkind (1988) calls the "imaginary audience." Because of this phenomenon, parents see adolescents agonizing for hours over what to wear or combing their hair so that it is perfect. Elkind maintains that females are more concerned than males with the imaginary audience. Try to be sympathetic about this heightened sensitivity rather than dismissing your child's concerns or behaviors as stupid and irrelevant. This stage will pass as adolescents formulate more abstract thinking skills and are able to look beyond themselves and assume a broader perspective.

Developing a sense of self is a complex task, and many important pieces need to fit to put the puzzle together. At this point, young adolescents are only embarking on the journey. They are still developing physically, mentally, socially, and emotionally. Remember that wearing certain clothes, trying out various hairstyles, listening to music that adults can't begin to appreciate, and hanging out with friends are all part of the process of arriving at a more concrete definition of self.

A Typical Self-Development Problem: Expressing Individuality

Remember what it was like to go shopping with your third grader? You picked out the clothes, your child was appreciative, and you thought the outfit you picked out looked great when your child wore it. For many parents, shopping with teenagers is a totally different story: They might not want to be seen shopping with you, they probably don't appreciate your suggestions, and you might not want to be seen with them wearing what they picked out! Battles about clothes and hairstyles are frequent during early adolescence. What should you do if your adolescent's dress or hairstyle doesn't meet your standards?

1. Decide if this is a major or minor problem. In the overall scheme of things, it is most likely a minor problem

that may become major if you insist on controlling the way the young person looks. You may *prefer* that your teenager not wear certain kinds of clothes, pierce one ear in three spots, or have a head shaved on one side, but is it worth the battle to *demand* it?

2. Keep in mind that the way your teenager looks isn't a reflection on you. Most other parents can appreciate what you are going through, and those who can't aren't worth worrying about. Most people have more important things to do than focus on how your teenager looks.

3. If the dress or hairstyle does seem extreme, work on some acceptable compromises. For example, during the week the teenager may wear whatever the school will allow, but for Sunday dinner at a restaurant, he or she will need to put on clean jeans and a shirt without holes. If the adolescent won't agree to that, he or she can choose not to go to Sunday dinner, but no activities with friends will be permitted during that time.

4. Take a deep breath—this is a phase that will pass. Ten years from now your adolescent probably won't be dressing this way. The choices he or she makes now are an important part of the search for identity.

SOCIAL DEVELOPMENT

If you are the parent of a young adolescent, you may be frustrated with the amount of time your teenager spends on the telephone. If you aren't frustrated, you are rare! While excessive phone use is a major concern for many parents, the phone is a lifeline to adolescents. Did you ever stop to think that phone conversations are safer than face-to-face encounters? Imagine wanting to find out if someone liked you. Wouldn't it be easier to do on the phone than in person? The phone can be a good way to practice the social skills adolescents need as relationships with peers assume high priority.

For the most part, young adolescents look to peers as a source of support. At the same time, they are very sensitive and vulnerable to peer humiliation. During this stage of development, adolescents' tendency to see themselves as at the center of the universe means they also tend to believe that others are as concerned about them as they are about themselves. As a result, they fantasize about how others will react to them. Because they are so sensitive to others' opinions, they tend to choose peers who are equal and similar. It is extremely important to them to dress like their friends, use the same type of speech, adopt the same superstar heroes, and listen to the same music. They do this to protect against disapproval, negative judgments, and put-downs.

As a result of this fear of rejection and need for approval, peer influence can be very strong. This is often a troublesome phenomenon for parents, who worry that their adolescent will become involved with drugs, alcohol, and sex in order to fit in. It may help to know that most adolescents choose friends whose behaviors, interests, and values are similar to theirs. In addition, peer influence can be positive. Depending on the group, there may be pressure to get good grades, to stay sober, or otherwise to be a "good kid."

Belonging is a significant factor during this period of development. A key issue for young adolescents is to be popular because being popular means that they are "somebody." Closely associated with the need to belong are the specific rules about how to behave and with whom to associate. This is when cliques emerge—the "preps," the "jocks," the "dirtheads," the "nerds." Each group has its own standards about what is or is not acceptable, and each sees itself as unique and special. Within the cliques, differences are discouraged. Members dress alike, develop their own in-jokes, and adopt similar attitudes about school and parents. Cliques reinforce sameness and give members a sense of self-worth. Still, there is a certain amount of inflexibility within these cliques: Once one is associated with a particular group, it is hard to switch because one's identity is attached to this group.

As adolescents get older, their friendships become closer. Adolescents often describe a friend as someone who understands their feelings, makes them feel better, and knows everything about them. A "best friend" is someone who is very close. Females tend to have more close, intimate friendships than males and are more likely to disclose personal information. In addition, females often experience more of the "fickle friend" phenomenon: Yesterday they were best friends, but today they are enemies. Many misunderstandings between friends develop because young adolescents still tend to interpret things very literally and are not yet able to step back and look at all sides of an issue before becoming upset. Parents can help their adolescents broaden their perspective by talking with them about other possible causes for such misunderstandings.

Believe it or not, between the ages of 11 and 13, young adoles-cents generally have more negative than positive feelings toward the opposite sex, depending in part on when pubertal changes occur. If dating occurs, it is usually done within the context of a group. Your adolescent may claim to be "going with" someone, but before you get too concerned, remember that his or her definition of "going with" is probably a lot different than yours! For most young adolescents, having a boyfriend or girlfriend means that they have someone to talk with on the phone and walk with to classes. It's probably wise not to waste energy worrying that the boyfriend or girlfriend will be the love of your teenager's life, because this is seldom the case.

A final comment about social development: Many parents wonder what normal parent-adolescent relationships are. First of all, it is normal for your adolescent to become less dependent on you. At the same time, he or she will feel ambivalent about the issue. Because of this ambivalence, some days your teenager will appear quite grown up and independent. There may even be angry outbursts if you try to control his or her behavior. Then, just when you think you are beginning to see a pattern, you may find your youngster cuddling up to you on the couch and acting mellow! This dichotomous behavior is just as confusing for ado-lescents as it is for parents. On the one hand, they resent parental control; on the other, they are afraid that their parents will abandon them if they are too grown up. It is a complex issue. Teenagers need their parents' reassurance that, even though their behavior may not always meet with approval, they are loved and accepted.

It is also very common for parents to assume that their ado-lescent doesn't need them or want anything to do with them. This is simply not the case. Most adolescents do want close rela-tionships. They also still need their parents, but in a different way than before. They may act as though they are embarrassed to be seen with their parents, but in reality they don't want their friends to think they are too dependent. They may insist that their friends' parents are more understanding than their own, but that is because their friends' parents aren't making the rules. They may act as though they don't care, but the majority of teenagers do care and try to earn their parents' approval. While there may be some strain on the relationship during adoles-cence, parents who understand adolescent development realize that this strain is in part due to the "letting go" process. Steinberg and Levine (1987) describe this process as a partnership in which the senior partner (the parent) has more expertise but is train-ing the junior partner (the adolescent) to take over the business of running his or her own life. Although the strain is difficult for parents, it helps to know it is an inevitable part of growing up.

A Typical Social Development Problem: Choosing Friends

A major concern many parents of adolescents share is that their teenager will be led astray by the wrong crowd. This is a particularly salient issue today, when there is more adolescent substance abuse, pregnancy, suicide, and violent behavior. Deciding whether or not to regulate friendships is a touchy issue. If you don't, bad things could happen, but if you do, you may very well intensify the conflict and create an intolerable home situation. What can you do?

1. Know your teen's friends and their parents. Encourage friends to spend time at your home so you can learn more about them. If your son or daughter asks to go to a party or spend the night, call the parents and verify the request. Your teenager may be angry about this and accuse you of a lack of trust. You can stress that your job as a parent is to make sure he or she is safe. Let the teenager know that if you are not permitted to call, he or she will not be allowed to go.

2. Analyze your specific concerns. Do you object to the friends because of the way they look? Are you sure you know whether or not they are serious students? Are you concerned because they have less parental supervision than you feel comfortable with? Do you know for a fact that they are smoking or drinking, or is this an assumption? It is best to check out the facts by asking discreet questions of school personnel, observing the friends during school activities, and learning more about them by having them spend time in your home. If your worst fears are confirmed, discuss with your adolescent what you know and why you are concerned. Do your best to avoid name-calling and stereotyping. Be prepared for rebuttals and rage—your teenager is likely to see your actions as interference. After sharing your concerns, express your hope that he or she will reevaluate the amount of time spent with these friends. Don't forbid contact unless you absolutely have to. The fact is, most teenagers do listen to their parents. If you can let this

be your teenager's decision, you will have less of the deceit and rebellion that could result in the very behavior you are trying to prevent.

3. Establish boundaries. If you disapprove of your son's or daughter's friends, you can prohibit him or her from going out with them, or you can try to police phone calls to them. However, unless you plan to be chained to your teenager's side, you cannot prevent contact at school. Although it is natural to be concerned about friendships, most teenagers will tell you that their friends mean more to them than anything. Consequently, if you prohibit contact your adolescent may lie and sneak around just to be with these friends. You could try establishing tighter restrictions with the less desirable friends and allowing the adolescent more freedom with others. Although it is probably not possible to avoid all power struggles in this area, letting the adolescent decide whom to associate with based on knowledge of greater or lesser restrictions may reduce some of the conflict. The bottom line is that it is important to evaluate whether tight control will achieve what you want.

EMOTIONAL DEVELOPMENT

If you are the parent of an 11- to 14-year-old, or know one, try completing the following checklist to describe this young person's characteristics.

	Yes	No	Sometimes
1. Appears happy and content.	☐	☐	☐
2. Is irritable for no particular reason.	☐	☐	☐
3. Appears apathetic.	☐	☐	☐
4. Gets defensive easily.	☐	☐	☐
5. Gets angry quickly, without warning.	☐	☐	☐
6. Becomes easily obsessed or preoccupied about a problem.	☐	☐	☐
7. Overreacts to criticism.	☐	☐	☐

	Yes	No	Sometimes
8. Has frequent mood swings (happy, sad, mad, etc.).	☐	☐	☐
9. Gets worried easily (about friends, appearance, performance, etc.).	☐	☐	☐
10. Appears "down" or depressed.	☐	☐	☐
11. Is easily frustrated.	☐	☐	☐
12. Is cheerful and pleasant to be around.	☐	☐	☐

To develop an emotional profile of your adolescent, take a look at your responses to Items 2 through 11. If you answered "yes" or "sometimes" to most or all of them, you may be questioning what is going on with your teenager and wondering whether he or she needs professional counseling. If you answered "no" to Items 1 and 12, you may be similarly concerned. However, it is important to stress that the behaviors described in Items 1 through 11 are characteristic of early adolescence and that young adolescents often are *not* happy or cheerful. To interpret your responses, you need to look at the total picture. In other words, until age 11, 12, or 13, was your son or daughter generally happy? For the most part, was he or she rarely frustrated, irritable, and depressed? Until recently, was your adolescent usually not defensive or overreactive? If so, it is very likely that you are now seeing the effects of the hormonal and physical changes that are turning your child's world upside down. In addition, if these mood changes started at about age 11, 12, or 13, you can be quite certain that they will begin to level out by age 15 or 16. If this leveling out doesn't happen, or if you begin to see a persistent pattern of depressed mood, irritability, anger, and hopelessness, you should by all means seek professional help. If the adolescent is experiencing extreme mood swings, antidepressant medication prescribed for a period of time may help. Counseling can also help both parents and teenager cope with the confusion and chaos that can result from such mood swings.

Along with rapid mood fluctuations, young adolescents often experience several other troublesome emotions—anxiety, shame, embarrassment, guilt, shyness, and confusion. As a result of so many negative emotions, many adolescents feel as if they are going crazy, and this can be very scary. However, because they feel very vulnerable if they admit how scared and confused they are, they often mask these feelings of fear and vulnerability with anger. Anger typically distances people and often results in increased conflict because parents fail to see the real feelings underneath. Take 14-year-old Christa, for example. Rather than talking to her parents about her jealousy of her older sister and her fear that her parents loved her sister more than they loved her, Christa mouthed back at every opportunity. In return, her parents grounded her to her room. At the same time, because her older sister wasn't talking back and was allowed to do things, Christa interpreted this as more favoritism and became increasingly angry. She convinced herself that no matter what she did she would never be as good or as loved as her sister, so she might just as well act "bad." Her parents continued to ground her, Christa continued to be belligerent, and they never did get to the heart of the problem.

As a parent, you may identify with this example. It may seem to you that your adolescent is deliberately trying to be as obnoxious as possible. Not only is this upsetting to you, but you may also think you would be remiss if you didn't address the misbehavior. On the other hand, if you attack the symptom without looking more carefully at what might be precipitating it, you could make matters worse. A good rule of thumb is to assume that your adolescent is not deliberately being defiant because it is enjoyable to do so. It is more likely that he or she is hurting and is expressing this feeling indirectly through anger or defiance.

It is easy to forget how powerful feelings are during early adolescence and how the slightest little thing can tip the scale. Remember that adolescents don't necessarily like feeling vulnerable and emotional. These feelings are as confusing for them as they are for you. Even though it may be hard for you to believe, most adolescents do feel guilty after intensely negative confrontations. Although they may have called you every name in the book during the period of intense anger, most of them don't really believe what they say. However, because of their shame, it is often very difficult for them to apologize. As a parent, you need to let your adolescent know that you won't tolerate verbal bashing. If your teenager cannot discuss the issue more calmly, ask him or her to leave the room. If the adolescent is too emotionally charged to do this, you should be the one to leave.

Keep in mind that other factors may be triggering angry outbursts. Is your family under stress? Has there been a recent death, divorce, or remarriage? Is there a "family secret," such as alcoholism or abusive behavior? If so, expect that confusion about these events will be expressed as anger, withdrawal, acting out, or depression. In these cases, professional counseling is needed to address the underlying issues.

Along with emotional turbulence, adolescents feel anxious about what is happening to them. Unfortunately, because many are still quite concrete in their thinking, they tend not to see alternative solutions. As a result, they don't always make the best choices about how to deal with their anxiety because they don't see that there are better options. For example, a parent recently shared that her daughter had been so afraid of giving a speech in front of the class that she had started skipping school rather than discuss the fear with her teacher. When she got in trouble for skipping the class, her shame increased, and she became even more anxious about how she would explain this to her parent.

The good news about early adolescence is that the emotional roller coaster will come to a stop. It is very common for this to happen just as suddenly as it began. The best advice to parents is to remember that if the emotional turmoil started during early adolescence, your teenager is in all probability experiencing the normal mood swings that characterize this stage of development. On the other hand, if your child was difficult prior to adolescence and you see the difficulty intensifying, you are dealing with more than normal adolescence and should consider professional help. Be aware that adolescent females generally experience more mood swings than males and tend to be more emotionally expressive and more sensitive to the emotional states of others. Males, on the other hand, experience more anger and contempt and are more likely to act out their feelings than to talk about them.

As a parent, understand that moodiness, sulking, and short tempers are an inherent part of early adolescence and that you may experience the brunt of this because your teenager knows that you will continue to love him or her no matter what. Although you should not tolerate rudeness and disrespect, it is important to be supportive instead of overreacting, lecturing, or criticizing.

A Typical Emotional Development Problem: Emotional Outbursts

"I hate you. You don't understand me. Why can't you be like Sandra's parents? They don't nag at her all the time, and they don't expect her to be perfect like you think I should be. Living in this house is like living in hell, and you are an absolute jerk."

To some of you, this kind of comment may be both familiar and painful. You may respond with tears or with anger. You don't understand why you deserve such verbal abuse, and you don't know how to handle it. What is even more confusing is that in a few minutes, you may experience a totally different child—one who is laughing, confiding in you, and acting as if the emotional outburst never happened. What should you do?

1. Remember that emotional outbursts are part of the normal upheaval associated with puberty. Do not personalize the attack because it is not meant to be personal. Recognize that this pushing away from you is part of the adolescent's process of becoming an individual. You will likely see more intense emotional "unloading" from adolescent females, particularly those who were very dependent as children. If you take note, you will probably also discover that the worst times correspond with menstruation.

2. Rather than respond in anger, do your best to ignore the verbal attack. After your adolescent has calmed down, explain that you are hurt and confused by the accusations and that you will leave the room when further episodes occur.

3. Invite discussion after things have calmed down. Be supportive. Even though at the time it may seem as though your teenager hates you, it is more likely that he or she is ashamed and doesn't know how to apologize. In some cases there is cause for underlying anger, but if you had a good relationship prior to adolescence, put this behavior in perspective and recognize it for what it is.

4. Suggest that your adolescent keep a journal or talk into a tape recorder when really upset. He or she can share this information with you if desired. More important, the writing or taping is a better and safer way to vent feelings than directing them at others.

CONCLUSION

Navigating through early adolescence is much easier if you remember a few key principles:

1. Many of the issues that arise during this period are about power and control. Teenagers are absolutely convinced that they do not want any controls and that they can get along perfectly well without them. Be advised that they do need controls and that these controls are a source of security. Your young adolescent may never admit this, but you need to believe it. Your adolescent probably won't thank you for your guidance, but leaving him or her to make decisions unassisted creates unacknowledged anxiety.

2. Much of what you construe to be disobedience is actually your teenager's way of asserting independence. If you are able to see the behavior in this way, it will change the way you deal with the problem, as illustrated by the following example: Kyle's father was angry because when he asked 14-year-old Kyle to mow the lawn, he expected it to be done right away. Kyle, on the other hand, saw nothing wrong with waiting several hours to do it because he had other things he wanted to do. After some discussion, the father understood that Kyle wasn't deliberately opposing him. He saw that part of Kyle's need as an adolescent was to begin making independent decisions and take more control of his life and his time. Kyle and his father were able to compromise on how and when chores should be done. Kyle explained to his dad that it wasn't that he hadn't intended to do the work, it was just that he wanted to be in charge of when. Obviously, some limits must be set for chore times, but understanding that resistance is related to the normal developmental task of assuming independence will make it easier to deal with the real issue.

3. Parents and teens will speak a different language for the next few years. For example, teenagers may interpret a simple request to put away the dishes as an attempt to structure their time. When you try to show interest in their activities or friends by asking how things are going, they may think you are prying. These language barriers can be frustrating, and there will be times when you think you need an interpreter!

4. Recognize that your teenager will make mistakes— and so will you. Think back to when your adolescent was a 2-year-old and wet the bed. Were you upset?

No, you probably realized that this was a normal part of toilet training. So when your adolescent spends his or her weekly allowance in one day, consider this within the context of learning how to adjust to increasing freedom. If necessary, you can help with money management techniques without making your teenager feel ashamed.

One last piece of advice: Appreciate the fact that your adolescent is maturing and trying out new behaviors. Don't panic and assume that what you see now is how he or she will be as an adult. There are still many more developmental challenges and changes, as you will read about in the next chapter.

6

Mid-Adolescence

Although the emotional upheaval of early adolescence usually lessens by mid-adolescence (ages 15 through 18), parents face a new set of challenges at this stage—how to handle their teenager's growing need for independence and how to "let go." Even though most parents don't fully realize it, their job is 60 to 80% over, and it is important to pull back slowly and begin allowing adolescents to handle things themselves. Because teenagers vary in their ability to assume this independence, it is difficult for parents to know how to pace this process. As one parent recalled, "I was just getting used to my son driving around town when he asked to take his first road trip to a city 100 miles away! I told him that I couldn't take giant steps . . . that it would take me a while to work up to that."

The difficulty arises in that many adolescents are convinced that their parents' job is 100% over and that they are capable of being in charge of everything. They tend to resent parental over-protection and "interference," as they call it. One adolescent heading off to college remarked to her mother, "Don't make me your summer project. I'm entirely capable of getting ready for college without your help."

Whether adolescents are or aren't ready to assume such independence isn't the issue. In their minds they are, and the more parents try to interfere, the more conflict occurs. In some cases, it seems as if the adolescent at this age is intentionally trying to create conflict. If it helps the youngster separate emotionally from his or her parents, this may indeed be the case.

Some parents who assumed that adolescence was forever are pleasantly surprised and relieved when their son or daughter begins to act more rational, is less intensely emotional, and can be seen in public with them! In general, despite the new issues that develop, mid-adolescence is an easier time than early adolescence.

To educate parents about mid-adolescence, our panel of adolescent "experts" came up with the following advice:

> "Let me make my own mistakes. If it's a bad one,
> so be it. I have to learn sometime."

> "Don't push too hard. If you do, I'll do the opposite."

> "Don't be totally lenient, but if you're too tight, I'm
> not going to know what to do when I move away
> from home."

> "Don't read too much into things; trust me."

> "Don't freak out if I want to dye my hair or wear
> weird clothes. That's just part of who I am."

> "Let me decide what's best for me."

> "Don't expect a full report when I walk in the door."

As a parent, you probably think this advice is just about as hard to follow or swallow as the advice the younger adolescents gave. As you reflect on these statements, you might consider just how horrible it is if adolescents express individuality by dying their hair or dressing at Goodwill. Just how terrible is it if they make some decisions that backfire and they have to face the consequences? Does it necessarily mean they don't love you just because they don't confide everything to you? You may come to realize that expressing individuality in the form of an off-the-wall hairstyle is better than doing it through sex or drugs. You may discover that adolescents learn some important lessons when they fall flat on their faces and that this will have greater impact than any lecture you might devise about driving too fast, skipping school, or the like. It's a fine line to walk and one that will be discussed in greater detail as we look at characteristics of mid-adolescence and what to do about typical problems.

CHARACTERISTICS OF MID-ADOLESCENCE

Some parents may recall a song Pat Boone sang, "Twixt Twelve and Twenty." In it, Boone implied that these were wonderful years— and they certainly can be. As a result of the physical changes that began in early adolescence, coupled with increased cognitive abilities, the adolescent at this age can think, feel, and behave in more complex, mature ways. If you are the parent of a 15- to 18- year-old, you may have some doubts about this statement because you don't see this maturity. Don't be discouraged; every teenager matures at his or her own pace. If you noticed changes in your young adolescent at about age 12, you will probably find that about age 15, he or she will be less moody and better able to confront issues without overreacting. However, if your child entered puberty later, you may continue to see many characteristics of the young adolescent in your 15- or 16-year-old. Although there is a lot of variation, you can rest assured that most parents find mid-adolescence less tumultuous than early adolescence.

During this developmental period, adolescents are less confident than they care to admit, and they often bolster their confidence through rebellion or defiance. They fear responsibility to some degree, yet know they can't remain dependent forever. Thinking about the future as an independent adult can be perplexing as well as exciting.

It is important to realize that there are some significant differences between teens and their parents during this stage of development. According to Thomas Phelan (1993), teenagers have more dreams than realities, and parents have more realities than dreams. Teenagers are excited about the unlimited possibilities for their future, seem to thrive on the turmoil in their lives, and spend a lot of time fantasizing about how great things will be. On the other hand, parents prefer stability over turmoil and have lived long enough to know that many of their own dreams as adolescents didn't come true. This is often a discouraging time for parents because they are living with the reality rather than the dream. In addition, because they were once teenagers, parents may overidentify with some of the issues evoked in a discussion of dreams and reality. For example, a mother who got pregnant at age 17 might have a difficult time listening to her 17-year-old daughter talk about the wonderful feeling of being in love without feeling scared herself. She might even project her fears onto her daughter as she thinks about her own dreams, which were never fully realized because of her early pregnancy.

Another difference is the marked disparity between parents who may be entering midlife and children who are in mid-adolescence. This disparity can result in a multitude of mixed feelings. For example, a mother is aware as she and her daughter walk down the street that the heads are turning because of her daughter, not because of her. While she may be proud of her daughter, she may also experience a sense of loss regarding her own physical attractiveness. A father may be envious of his adolescent's energy and strength because he isn't able to do as many physical things as easily as when he was younger. Parents need to be aware of their own feelings and work on resolving such issues.

A third difference is that while you as a parent are investing in your child, your child is investing in his or her peers. It is sometimes distressing for parents to accept this reality, and sometimes bad feelings develop because parents feel they are running a hotel and paying the expenses while their teenagers come and go as they please. Many of the conflicts that occur at this age revolve around relationships with peers or the amount of time spent with them.

A fourth difference is a major one: Teens want to be on their own, and parents are struggling to let go. The extent to and manner in which an adolescent pushes depends partly on that particular adolescent's personality, but unless parents want the child to stay home forever, they must gradually let go of the reins. Try to appreciate the fact that your adolescent's musical listening habits and tastes are different from yours or that he or she thinks it's cool to have a nose ring and live in a messy room. It's all about independence. As one 17-year-old girl stated, "I'm going to do what I'm going to do, and there's nothing you can really do about it." This was probably wishful thinking on her part, but when teens reach this age, parents do have to decide what they can most easily let go of.

Following are descriptions of physical, intellectual, self-, social, and emotional development during mid-adolescence. Knowledge of the characteristics of this period of development will help you understand what you can expect. Examples of typical problems, including specific suggestions for resolving them, are also described.

PHYSICAL DEVELOPMENT

Depending on when the young adolescent begins puberty, physical development during mid-adolescence may continue at a rather rapid rate or gradually begin to slow down. By age 15, most females have started to menstruate and have achieved nearly full breast growth. Their body weight has been redistributed, which results in a more fully developed figure. Females tend to be dissatisfied with their bodies, and it is during early and mid-adolescence that parents need to be on the alert for signs of eating disorders such as anorexia (obsessive avoidance of food) and bulimia (uncontrollable binging and vomiting). Chapter 7 describes these eating disorders in more detail.

Although males lag behind females in development, by mid-adolescence they are finally the same height as their female peers. By age 15 their voices have started to lower; facial hair begins to appear by age 16.

Keep in mind that these ages are approximations and vary according to each adolescent. Genes, nutrition, and the current trend toward experiencing puberty earlier than in previous generations all affect physical maturation.

Sexual urges are very strong during mid-adolescence. Statistics indicate that by the time they graduate from high school, half of today's teenagers will have had intercourse (Steinberg & Levine, 1990). Sexual activity may have been the exception rather than the rule when you were a teenager, but your teenager may see intimate sexual relationships as very normal and healthy. If you look at the statistics, you can see he or she is not alone. As a parent, you might like to hide your head in the sand, but the reality is that your adolescent may be in the half of the graduating class that has or will have had intercourse. Rather than waste energy fighting this reality, it is more important than ever that you take an active role in helping your teenager be sexually responsible. This is not to say that you must condone your youngster's sexual behavior; however, it is important to realize that teenagers need accurate information about the responsibilities of a sexual relationship and guidance on avoiding pressure to be sexually active. They also need to know the facts about pregnancy, birth control, and sexually transmitted diseases, including AIDS.

Sexuality evokes considerable anxiety for adolescents and their parents. In particular is the concern about sexual orientation. Although sexual orientation is actually determined at an early age, it is during this period that teens begin to experiment with sexual behavior and deal with their feelings. Because of the lack of support for gay and lesbian adolescents, they are at high risk for suicide. Parents need to understand the conflict homosexuality can create for the adolescent and seek professional counseling for themselves and their adolescent if negative parental feelings get in the way of dealing realistically with the issue.

Although it may feel awkward for you to discuss sexuality, it is imperative that you do. Remember that most teenagers are not obsessed with sex and most do not have intercourse on a regular basis. However, that isn't to say they won't try it, in part because trying out more grown-up roles is one thing this period of development is about. Therefore, adolescents need to know the facts as well as the risks and how to minimize them. Although you cannot control your teenager's ultimate decision regarding sexual activity, you can control the quality of the information he or she receives. That in turn can have a positive impact on your adolescent's behavior.

A Typical Physical Development Problem: Sexual Involvement

From a parent's perspective, it's easy to tell your adolescent, "Just say no to sex." But for an adolescent who is just beginning to experience sexual feelings and explore intimate relationships, it is not that simple. Some adolescents feel more like adults if they have had intercourse. For others, sex is a status symbol, a way of achieving prestige and acceptance. Furthermore, while many teenagers realize that relationships at this stage are temporary, they do not think there is anything wrong with having sex if you are going with someone, or they may not think a relationship is very meaningful if it doesn't include sex.

The pressure is strong to be sexually active before adolescents are emotionally ready to handle the involvement. There no longer seems to be a negative stigma attached to early sexual activity. What should you do if you suspect sexual activity or want to prevent it?

1. Do not preach about how wrong it is to have sex. Adolescents will tune you out because they think they are old enough to make this decision themselves. If you tell them they should wait until marriage, they will probably call you old-fashioned because they know that most people don't wait until marriage. They may assume that they can't talk to you about sex if you have this attitude.

2. Initiate frank, open discussions, keeping in mind that many teenagers still subscribe to the personal fable that "It can happen to everyone else but not to me."

That is one reason why so many adolescents end up pregnant. They didn't take precautions because they didn't think it was necessary. In addition, adolescents' sense of time can still be pretty immediate. They live in the present, and it is difficult for them to think of long-term consequences. At this point they also have more dreams than reality, so getting pregnant and having a baby may seem pretty neat. You need to help your teenager see the risks involved with sexual activity and explore the characteristics and realities of meaningful relationships and commitment.

3. As you talk, gently ask about what your adolescent really knows. Another reason many adolescents fail to use birth control regularly is that they don't have accurate facts about pregnancy and sexually transmitted diseases. It is important for you to know the facts as well. Check your local library or bookstore for up-to-date information.

4. If your teenager shares with you that he or she has been sexually active, or if you suspect this to be the case, don't take risks yourself. Discuss the wisdom of using birth control, including the use of condoms to prevent AIDS and other sexually transmitted diseases. This certainly doesn't imply that you are saying, "Do as you please." You may think you are encouraging sexual activity if you discuss birth control, but in reality you are discouraging sexual irresponsibility. It is better for everyone to be safe than sorry.

INTELLECTUAL DEVELOPMENT

Formal operational thinking continues to develop during the period of mid-adolescence, even though many people do not achieve it until much later in life. The degree to which teens have moved into this more advanced level of thinking significantly affects how they think and behave. Specifically, as they develop the ability to think more abstractly, they are better able to hypothesize about the future. As a result, they are less likely to conceptualize everything in either-or terms. They acquire the ability to distinguish the real and concrete from the hypothetical and abstract, and are capable of pondering and philosophizing, particularly about moral, social, and political issues. They may take up causes, perhaps joining an organization of students against drunk driving or working to protect children from abuse.

Another change in intellectual ability allows youngsters in mid-adolescence to use organizational strategies more effectively. As a parent, you may doubt this, especially when you look at the chaos in your teenager's room or the way he or she manages time! However, to adolescents this way of organizing probably makes sense. Many of them have very busy schedules to coordinate, involving school, work, and other activities. Although you might not think it is a good idea to start doing homework at 10:00 P.M., making this choice reflects the development of a sense of organization without adult supervision. Adolescents will be leaving home in a very short time and need to practice this skill.

Although their reasoning abilities are improving, adolescents at this stage are far from perfect. At some times they may seem more logical than at others. Although they may have the capacity to see alternatives, they still may lack the experience and self-understanding to make appropriate choices. As a result, they sometimes act confused or make foolish decisions. This tendency upsets parents. "Why," questioned one father, "can my son be very logical and responsible about anything related to his car, but he doesn't have the common sense to turn on the sprinkler when he sees the lawn burning up?" The answer? For one thing, his car matters to him and is a symbol of his world. The lawn, on the other hand, is not as personally relevant.

You may also see discrepancies in your adolescent's level of abstract thinking when it comes to future plans. Many parents are frustrated because of their adolescent's failure to set long-term goals or make plans for after high school. In reality, adolescents are probably not able to do this if they are still relatively concrete in their thinking. The best they can do is to look at short-range goals until their higher level thinking skills develop more completely. To avoid frustration about these issues, try reframing situations by remembering how it was when your adolescent was 5 years old and learning how to tie shoes. You probably didn't expect perfection on the first try. Because more advanced thinking skills don't pop up overnight, you must also be patient now.

If you live with an adolescent between the ages of 15 and 18, you are well aware that youngsters at this stage can be argumentative with very little provocation. They will question rules, demand explanations, and respond with sophisticated counterarguments. An all too typical conversation might sound like this.

Parent: You need to be home by 11:00 P.M. tonight.

Teenager: Why? I don't have to get up early tomorrow.

Parent: No, but I do, and until you are home, I can't get to sleep.

Teenager: Well, that's your problem. I shouldn't be punished for something you can't do.

Sound familiar? Sometimes parents of teenagers long for the days of middle childhood, when their children idolized them and accepted what they said without rebuttal!

On the positive side, it can be stimulating to have adult conversations with your adolescent. You may be amazed at how well your son or daughter can articulate complex ideas. You must also remember to keep your sense of humor when your adolescent thinks he or she knows more about an issue than you do. Rather than arguing your point to win, just appreciate the experience of engaging in a philosophical discussion and relish the opportunity to see your child's intellect unfold. Recognize that there will be loopholes in the logic but that such loopholes are part of the process.

A Typical Intellectual Development Problem: Questioning Family Values, Beliefs, and Practices

If you are living with an adolescent, you are used to your son or daughter trying to convince you that he or she knows what is best. And because you might have a very different opinion of what is best, conflict occurs. There are no easy solutions when you find your values, beliefs, and practices challenged, and you may struggle with how to allow your adolescent to learn to think independently and at the same time not allow total rejection of your core values and principles.

What should you do when you find your teenager challenging your opinions and questioning or rejecting family values and practices as part of his or her intellectual maturation?

1. First, realize that adolescents sometimes challenge just to test your reaction. They may not be totally convinced themselves about their position, but they are trying the waters and testing you out. If you overreact and make a big deal of it, it will become a big deal. It is

best to hear your adolescent out, state your position as calmly as possible, and look at ways to compromise.

2. Decide which issues are worth doing battle over. If going to church or on family vacations is something you do not want to budge on, consider giving in when your teenager questions why he or she must continue taking music lessons. Even though you would like to see the lessons continue, it might be easier to admit that your child's interests have changed and realize that the skill can be resumed later in life.

3. Don't be too surprised if your adolescent accuses you of being hypocritical, biased, or uninformed. At the same time, don't get your feathers ruffled over it. More advanced abstract thinking skills allow your adolescent to see that you sometimes preach one thing and practice another. He or she may likewise find that viewpoints accepted without question during childhood no longer fit as he or she grows older and knows more. If you don't take such questioning personally, you can probably avoid a great deal of confrontation.

4. Be prepared for subtle changes. Your teenager may begin to drink coffee, adopt different mannerisms to accompany a particular identity, or develop ideas that parallel the thoughts expressed in music or by peers. Don't assume that these will be permanent changes—teens are still exploring what they believe.

SELF-DEVELOPMENT

Dear, dear! How queer everything is today! And yesterday things went on just as usual. I wonder if I've been changed in the night? Let me think: Was I the same when I got up this morning? I almost think I can remember feeling a little different. But if I'm not the same, the next question is, "Who in the World am I?" Ah, that's the puzzle! (Carroll, 1971, pp. 15–16)

Just like Alice in Lewis Carroll's classic *Alice in Wonderland*, 15- to 18-year-olds are trying to answer the question "Who am I?" Along with achieving independence, preoccupation with one's identity is a primary task at this stage of development. The process of finding oneself at this age involves establishing a sexual, vocational, political, social, moral, and religious identity. Adolescents do this by trying on various roles and responsibilities, engaging in discussions, observing peers and adults, speculating about possibilities with their friends, and doing a lot of self-questioning, experimenting, and exploring. Unless they have tried on different ways of looking, thinking, acting, and being, they cannot know who they really are. Parents who are concerned about the amount of time teenagers spend in their rooms alone listening to music, talking on the phone with friends, or doing "nothing" need to understand that all this is a valuable part of the identity search.

While young adolescents looked like carbon copies of the other members of their particular peer group, by mid-adolescence youngsters are generally more self-confident and are beginning to establish themselves as individuals within a group. This is why you will see them dying their hair green if everyone else's is red and wearing Salvation Army attire when their friends are wearing designer clothes. Although expressing their individuality through their clothing and appearance might not seem all that significant, this self-assertion extends to other areas as well. Depending on their degree of self-confidence, adolescents at this stage are much more capable of resisting peer pressure. This self-assurance, coupled with increased abilities to look beyond the immediate and speculate about long-term consequences, makes it easier for them to say no when it comes to situations where their values are being challenged.

This doesn't mean there won't be some experimentation in areas where parents feel most uncomfortable—sex and alcohol. Consider the following scenario.

Parent: We know you were drinking last night. We are surprised and upset that you would do this.

Teenager: Well, I'm 17, and this was the first time. A whole lot of my friends do it. I just needed to know what it was like—not because they do it, but because I can't make a decision not to drink if I've never tried it. Now I know that it's not something I want to do, even if everyone else does. You'll just have to trust me.

Although as a parent you might not buy this logic, it does make sense to teenagers. As illustrated by this scenario, the issue is not peer pressure but rather trying out a behavior to see how it fits one's self-perceptions.

Adolescents at this stage are less self-conscious and less concerned with their image than before. They no longer assume that the whole world is focused on them, and they are less likely to experiment with eccentric behaviors simply to evoke a negative response, even though they may engage in them as part of their identity search.

As adolescents look in the mirror, they see they are no longer children but question who they will be as adults. As part of the quest for identity, parents can expect to see their teenagers changing interests, plans, and friends. A son or daughter who has taken piano lessons since first grade now decides to give them up. Friendships may change—the adolescent may drift into the "party crowd" or begin to associate strictly with the athletes. The adolescent may assume different mannerisms or be obsessive about his or her appearance, needing to dress to complement a particular role.

Anxiety and confusion are often part of the identity search. As thinking becomes more sophisticated, adolescents are able to see that many of their childhood fantasies might not work in real life. There is a certain amount of loss associated with this developmental stage as adolescents look at who they really are, what they want in life, and how they can achieve these goals.

A Typical Self-Development Problem: What Should I Be?

During this stage of development, adolescents experience increasing pressure to define who they are and what they want to do when they grow up. For many, this is a perplexing question because their sense of time is still fairly immediate and it is difficult for them to project into the future. Parents become frustrated because they do not see a commitment in one direction, but a tentative drifting from one thing to another. Both adolescents and parents feel compelled to "figure it out" because there aren't many more years of high school left.

What should you do if your adolescent seems confused and directionless about his or her identity and future?

1. Relax. Even though your teenager will be graduating from high school, that doesn't necessarily mean he or she has to have it all figured out. Some adolescents are less mature than others and need more time to sort things through. For some, this won't happen until they are in their early to mid-20s. There is a lot of societal pressure on you and your teenager to have a plan.

While it would be nice to have that, it may be premature to push it.

2. Recognize that part of the dilemma may be that some adolescents lack self-confidence and are afraid to graduate and leave the security of home and high school behind. If you sense that this is the case for your son or daughter, initiate some discussion about the issue and help your teenager look realistically at strengths and weaknesses, clarify any misconceptions he or she may have about what you expect, and confront fears. Stress that it is normal to feel anxious—leaving home for the first time is a major life transition. Acknowledge that it may be hard to leave friends, that there can be sadness in knowing that nothing will be the same again, and that it is natural to worry about making new friends, achieving adequately in a job or in school, or being able to make enough money to live independently. At the same time, try to get in touch with and deal with how your child feels about this transition.

3. Be sure your adolescent is scheduled to take the aptitude and interest tests that are generally provided as part of the school counseling curriculum. In addition, work with the school counselor to arrange job shadowing experiences or mentoring opportunities to help clarify your adolescent's future direction.

SOCIAL DEVELOPMENT

Because adolescents are still striving for social acceptance during mid-adolescence, peers continue to play an important role. Teenagers prefer friends to family because friends don't make as many demands, don't impose limits, and can be chosen and dropped at will. Friends don't require the laundry to be folded or complain that too many miles have been put on the car! With peers, adolescents can try out various roles, learn to tolerate individual differences as they come in contact with people who have different values and life-styles, and prepare themselves for adult interactions as they begin to develop intimate relationships.

If the adolescent has attained formal operational thinking, relationships will be more mature and less focused on activities. While friends still continue to be a very important source of emotional support, by age 17 there is often less need for a confidant and someone to depend on. This in turn increases the ability to appreciate people with differing characteristics.

Parents may also see closer relationships with a few friends rather than obsessive concern about being part of a clique. More self-assured adolescents will associate with a wider variety of peers and will not be as anxious about being included. Once they have reached the developmental milestone symbolized by the driver's license, they are more mobile and can initiate contacts with teenagers in nearby communities. This can be a source of anxiety to parents because it becomes more difficult for them to know their teenager's friends.

Attachments to the opposite sex grow stronger, and some competition may develop as adolescents vie for boyfriends or girlfriends. Many will form exclusive relationships with someone of the opposite sex. Females tend to develop romantic interests earlier than males, and they also suffer more disillusionment when the realities of an intimate relationship do not match up with their fantasy of romance. Sexual experimentation usually does not begin until mid-adolescence. As noted previously, adolescents begin to clarify their sexual orientation at this time.

Teenagers in mid-adolescence are more likely to resent parents' questions about where they are going or whom they are going to be with. They don't like to have their time scheduled or activities planned. Much of their socializing occurs on the spur of the moment. Therefore, their parents' attempts to clarify the social calendar often fall on deaf ears.

Depending on the adolescent's level of maturity, relationships with parents tend to be less volatile, and family interaction is more positive. During early adolescence, relationships with siblings were often conflicted. The 15- to 18-year-old is better able to give and take, so sibling relationships are also more harmonious.

Parents continue to be an important source of support and role-modeling. Adolescents need their parents' experience and guidance as they make important decisions about their future. Parents serve as a "safety net." Although they might not admit it, most teenagers feel more secure knowing there is someone to rely on.

A Typical Social Development Problem: Romantic Involvement

Like it or not, your adolescent may fall in love at least once during high school. It is important to see these romantic relationships for what they are and to recognize that most of them don't result in lifetime partnerships. Nevertheless, an intense romance usually provokes anxiety for adolescents and their parents, albeit for different reasons.

For adolescents, issues of trust, jealousy, commitment, and sexual feeling are dominant. Parents worry about unhealthy, dependent relationships; sexual involvement; the values of the person their adolescent is dating; and the amount of time their youngster spends with this individual.

Suppose you are concerned about the person your son or daughter is involved with because of the family's background or the person's values or behavior. Or perhaps you feel that the person is a negative influence on your son or daughter or see the relationship as too serious and controlling. What can you do?

1. Remember that the more you try to control whom your adolescent can and cannot see, the more attractive the forbidden individual may seem. Continuing to see the person may be your adolescent's way of letting you know that you are not in control. Therefore, think twice before you forbid your son or daughter to associate with someone. In addition, try to pinpoint what you find objectionable and what you actually know for a fact about this person. You may assume that the person will be a bad influence, but where is the evidence for that? If your adolescent shows signs of antagonistic, rebellious behavior when prior to the relationship no such signs existed, you may be correct in assuming that the person is having an undesirable influence. On the other hand, take care not to blow the situation out of proportion and make it more of an issue than it really is.

2. Using effective communication techniques, express your concerns to your adolescent. Be careful not to attack the other person. As objectively as possible, point out the changes you have seen in your son or daughter and your concerns about your teenager's spending so much time with the boyfriend or girlfriend rather than with other friends, the possessive nature of the relationship, or sexual involvement and the consequences of that. Expect rebuttal, but try not to argue. Keep focusing on your feelings by delivering good "I" messages. Although your son or daughter may not admit it at the time, if you have had a relatively

close, respectful relationship, he or she may very well be listening to what you have to say but won't want to admit that you may be right. As a parent, you must realize that sometimes the best way for both you and your adolescent to learn is through experience, painful as it may be.

3. If the relationship is truly objectionable and you have good reason to think that it is detrimental to your teenager's well being, you may decide to establish some boundaries. For example, although you cannot keep your teenager from seeing the person at school, you can prohibit the person from attending family functions, riding in your car, or coming to your house. You can be clear with your teenager that you do not approve of the person and do not condone the relationship. If you take these measures, be aware that doing so may encourage lying and deceitful behavior.

4. Recognize that no magic solution exists for this type of problem. Parents understandably worry about their teenagers' relationships, and the more unhealthy the relationship, the more that concern increases. As a parent, you may want to talk with your teenager about the differences between healthy and unhealthy relationships and emphasize the negative aspects of becoming too dependent; allowing another person to control one's thoughts, feelings, and behaviors; keeping feelings bottled up inside or expressing them aggressively; and not having a healthy sense of self.

EMOTIONAL DEVELOPMENT

Most parents begin to breathe a sigh of relief when they discover that their adolescent is beginning to develop more emotional stability. Depending on the rate of maturation, adolescents at this age are less likely to have full-blown temper tantrums, complete with out-of-control behavior and verbal abuse. Parents are also less likely to see rapid mood fluctuations because adolescents are becoming less overwhelmed by their emotions. As a result, they can handle emotionally charged issues more adeptly. If your adolescent is late in maturing, you can expect the same characteristics as described for the young adolescent, but knowing that there is smoother sailing ahead may help you through this period.

Because they do not feel as vulnerable, 15- to 18-year-olds tend to be less defensive. They are more capable of expressing their emotions and working through problems and less likely to act out their emotions behaviorally. This is not to say that all adolescents have this capability. The disturbing fact about this stage of development is that adolescents can act unpredictably because of lags in their level of maturity. It may seem confusing that the adolescent seems more emotionally stable yet overreacts in certain situations. The situation next described illustrates the problem.

Sixteen-year-old Todd had been dating his girlfriend for several months. They had experienced their ups and downs, but on the whole, he seemed to be handling the relationship reasonably well. This is why his parents were so surprised that he became depressed and expressed suicidal thoughts when his girlfriend hadn't called when she said she would and had chosen to spend most of the weekend with her girlfriends rather than with him. When they were finally able to get him to talk about it, Todd expressed fear that because his girlfriend didn't call when she said she would and spent the weekend with her girlfriends, this meant she was losing interest in the relationship. He also assumed that he would never feel this way about anyone again. With his parents' support, Todd was able to work through his feelings, and his parents learned that he probably would not handle all situations with the same degree of emotional maturity.

Many adolescents, particularly seniors in high school, feel lonely. They may be gradually growing away from their friends as their interests and beliefs change. Because many adolescents at this stage are becoming involved in more significant dating relationships, those who aren't may feel different, isolated, and lonely.

Ambivalence also characterizes this period of development. On the one hand, teens may look forward to leaving high school and embarking on a new life. On the other hand, they may be apprehensive about the future. Self-doubt and insecurity may also result if they realize they don't have the skills, ability, or requirements needed for a job, postsecondary education, or the military. These feelings may heighten as they compare themselves with classmates who do have these skills and abilities.

Although anger is usually not as common during mid-adolescence as in early adolescence, parents of high school seniors may be wise to recognize that it is easier for some to separate and leave home if they are angry. In other words, so they won't feel as vulnerable, some teens create conflict to make it easier to distance themselves from home and family.

The good news at this stage is that most, though not all, adolescents are more likely to verbalize their feelings than to act them out. It is important for parents to encourage the expression of feelings. By doing so, they can develop a better understanding of what is going on with their teenager.

A Typical Emotional Development Problem: Dealing with Ambivalence and Confusion

Think back to when you were 16, 17, or 18 years old. Do you remember all the choices you suddenly had? Although your parents may still have been a primary influence, ultimately you were the one who had to decide whether or not to:

Do well in school

Stay in a relationship or ask someone for a date

Drink or smoke

Be sexually active

Obey the speed limit and other laws

Tell your parents the truth about where you were or whom you were with

Get a job, continue your education, or go into the military

Drop out of school

Participate in extracurricular activities and, if so, which ones

Tell on a friend

The list could go on and on. Your adolescent is faced with these same choices, and, in certain cases, the choices are more difficult because the norms of our culture have changed. When you reflect on the sheer number of choices, it is easy to see how confusing this period can be. Values are tested, and beliefs are challenged.

As a parent, what should you do to help your adolescent deal with confusion and ambivalence?

1. Encourage communication by being supportive and listening. Don't push for solutions. Instead, try to get your teenager to discuss his or her feelings with you, a friend, or a counselor.

2. If possible, help your adolescent sort out the real issues. Is she confused about going out for the volleyball team because of fear of failure? Is he unsure about what to do after high school because he feels pressure from you about what he *should* do? It is important to work through such questions to clarify the problem, deal with the issue, and arrive at a decision.

3. Don't moralize or preach about smoking, drinking, sex, school performance, or obeying the law. However, state your position on these issues and help your adolescent identify long- and short-term consequences of various choices. At this stage, your teenager needs to be able to make decisions independently—you can't keep him or her under lock and key forever. It is understandable that you are anxious about giving up control; in reality, so are a lot of teenagers. That's why it is advisable to be as supportive as you can when your teenager shares his or her confusion with you.

4. Sometimes adolescents think they have to figure things out for themselves and that they are wimps if they ask for help or admit to feeling confused or ambivalent. If you remember to put yourself in your teenager's shoes, you can occasionally verbalize what you think the confusion at the center of the conflict is—for example, "I've noticed that you haven't been going out with your boyfriend lately. Are you trying to decide whether or not to stay in this relationship?" An open invitation such as this may be the encouragement your adolescent needs to sort through the confusion.

CONCLUSION

You may recall the words to the Cat Stevens song "Father and Son." In these poignant lyrics, a father tells his son that it's hard to keep all the things he knows inside, but that he realizes that if he were to give advice, his son would turn away. He lets his son know that he was once young and therefore knows it's not easy to grow up. He cautions his son about making changes too fast, acknowledging that he has a lot to go through and encouraging him to speculate about his dreams. He concludes with the words "I know I have to go."

This song captures the essence of mid-adolescence for both teenagers and parents. It acknowledges that growing up is a challenge and that adolescents need to learn to cope with the difficult experiences that are part of life. It also addresses the struggle parents have in the letting go process and concludes with the inevitable: Parents need to step back and let their adolescents prepare themselves to meet the demands of the adult world.

This process is more difficult for some parents than for others. You have probably heard some parents say, "I can't wait until my kids graduate from high school and are on their own." You may know other parents who want to hang on as long as they can. These different perspectives no doubt reflect the quality of the parent-adolescent relationship during these last several years.

This stage of life contains two major developmental markers—getting a driver's license and graduating from high school. Independence characterizes both events. In the interim, adolescents will slip, stumble, and fall. However, as they make their mistakes and celebrate their successes, they are learning important skills that will carry them into young adulthood.

As a parent, hang on to these key principles:

1. Even though adolescents imply that you should get out of their lives, very few really mean that in a complete sense. While your adolescent may reject your advice or opinions right now, this does not mean that a few years down the road he or she won't appreciate your perspective. Remember that this is a stage; when it passes, your adolescent may end up a lot like you!

2. Don't let go all at once. Adolescents are not yet mature, even though they are striving to be. It is best for parents to take baby steps. When your teen has proven he or she can handle responsibility, your anxiety will decrease and you will be ready to move to the next level. Don't assume there won't be setbacks, because there will be. Just when you think you trust your teenager and things are going well, he or she may blow it. That is disappointing but usually not devastating. Just regroup and get back on track.

3. Try not to get defensive. Help your adolescent channel the rebellious push for independence, but don't condemn it. If you want your teenager to develop into a mature, independent adult capable of respect for authority and for the rights and needs of others, he or she must be given increasing opportunities to venture out.

4. Develop some emotional muscle. When your adolescent starts to push you away, realize that these behaviors are developmental, not personal. Keep things in perspective: Don't assume the worst or make a mountain out of a molehill.

In conclusion, try to enjoy watching your adolescent bloom. Just as with other stages, mid-adolescence is finite. These are most likely the last years you will have the opportunity on a regular basis to observe and experience your child's cognitive, emotional, social, physical, and self-development changes. Enjoy as much of it as you can!

7

....

When the Problems Don't Seem So Normal

The previous chapters have focused on many issues, including parenting stages and styles, communication and discipline techniques, and normal development from preschool through middle adolescence. At this point, it is time to stop and ask yourself what you have learned. To answer that question, we invite you to take the following quiz. Just check off your responses to the following true-false questions.

	True	False
1. Perfect parents do exist.	☐	☐
2. Parents should know the answers to all the issues related to child rearing.	☐	☐
3. If you want to have a positive relationship with your child or adolescent, an authoritarian parenting style is best.	☐	☐
4. Adolescents in particular respond well to lecturing, advice, and criticism.	☐	☐
5. Using logical consequences generally works better than using punishment.	☐	☐

	True	False
6. Imaginative play is characteristic of preschoolers	☐	☐
7. You can expect growth and development to be more stable during middle childhood than in early adolescence.	☐	☐
8. Young adolescents are generally not irritable, moody, or self-conscious.	☐	☐
9. During middle adolescence, you are likely to see teenagers trying to express their individuality and clarifying their identity in a variety of interesting ways.	☐	☐
10. Raising children is always easy.	☐	☐

Let's see how you did. If you checked "false" for Items 1, 2, 3, 4, 8, and 10, and "true" for 5, 6, 7, and 9, you have learned a lot about parenting!

WHAT TO DO WHEN YOU THINK THE PROBLEM IS SERIOUS

We've already talked about the normal ways children grow. In this final chapter, we will address some not-so-normal problems. As you were reading the previous chapters, you may have had some concerns about your son or daughter that were not necessarily allayed by the information you have read. For example, you might think that your third grader's impulsivity and inability to sit still don't match what you understand to be the norm. You may intuitively sense that your adolescent daughter's mood swings are extremely intense, and when she mentions that she wishes she were dead, your better judgment tells you this is definitely not characteristic of normal development.

Numerous problems could have been described in this chapter, but we chose those for which specific identifiable signs and symptoms could be listed. The problems specifically described include Attention Deficit Hyperactivity Disorder (ADHD), suicide, depression, delinquent behavior, eating disorders, drug and alcohol abuse, sexual abuse, and cult activity.

As you read the signs and symptoms of these problems, a warning light may come on in your head. If this is the case, here is some strong advice:

1. Do not become emotionally overwhelmed. This advice is easier to give than to take—when you see that your child or adolescent has a serious problem, it is natural for your emotions to take control. You are probably very worried and wonder whether things will ever be all right again. Or you may ask if there will be severe long-term consequences. You might feel angry about your son's or daughter's behavior, the situation, and the effect on you and others. You may resent the fact that you have to deal with the problem and that it will take time, money, and energy. You could be thinking, "Why my kid? Why our family?" You might feel guilty, believing you should have been able to prevent the problem. Perhaps you feel ashamed and concerned about what others will think or say about your child and your family. In addition, hopelessness, helplessness, and powerlessness are common feelings. Despite the problem, it is important for you to get a handle on your emotions so they don't get in the way of your ability to take action.

   How do you do this? First, recognize that while you would prefer not to have to deal with this issue, the reality is that a problem exists. However, the problem is not a reflection on you: You are not a bad parent, and your child or adolescent is not a bad kid. Second, don't worry about what others may be thinking or saying. You can't do much about that, and worrying won't help solve the problem. Third, keep telling yourself that there are numerous sources of help for these kinds of problems, that things can get better, and that you are not alone—many parents and kids are in similar situations. Fourth, seek professional counseling to deal with *your* emotions.

2. Remember that kids need love and acceptance at times when you think they least deserve it. Although it may be hard for you to be supportive, you need to keep communicating your love for your child and your concern about what is happening. Depending on the circumstances and your degree of emotional control,

this could be difficult. However, especially at times
like these, your child needs to know you care.

3. Get professional help for your child and/or family.
Most of the problems described in this chapter are far
too difficult to try to solve yourself. Rather than go it
alone, seek family counseling and help from support
groups. Some parents don't do this because they are
embarrassed to ask for help, think their child won't
like or benefit from it, or feel they can't afford it. Don't
be embarrassed to ask for help because now is the
time you need it. Think about it this way: If you had a
bad case of the flu, you would go to the doctor or get
some medicine. What's wrong with getting help if the
problem is emotional or behavioral rather than physical?
Don't assume that your child has to like going to
counseling or that it won't do any good. Do not give
your child the power to decide if he or she will or
will not go to counseling—that should be a parental
decision. Carefully check out the professionals in your
area and select one who has a good reputation for
working with children, adolescents, and families.
Finally, most communities have some agencies with
sliding fee scales to help on the financial end. And it
costs nothing to get help from support groups or from
school counselors, psychologists, or social workers.

4. Do not expect the problem to disappear overnight or
think that changing it will be an easy process. With
some problems, there is a great deal of denial, on the
child's as well as the parents' part. You will be far more
successful in resolving the problem if you acknowledge
its reality and put your energy into working on solutions
than if you try to convince yourself that this can't be
happening, that it's just a phase and will pass, or that
it's not that much of a problem.

5. Take care of yourself. During times of stress, it is easy
for parents to lose confidence or to have disagreements
with friends, spouses, or other family members about
how to handle the situation. If one parent denies the
situation and the other wants to confront it, the marital
relationship can suffer. In fact, the marital relationship
can be negatively affected even if both parents totally
agree. In single-parent families, the stress level can be
very high because there may be only one person to

cope with the problem and no one else in the house for support. To take care of yourself, get out of the situation periodically, look for support groups or family and friends who can be there for you, don't bottle up your feelings, and don't give up all sources of enjoyment and pleasure.

6. Do not give up hope. Tough times don't last forever. With the appropriate support and resources, things can change for the better. But if you keep pretending the problem doesn't exist, things could get a lot worse. The problems discussed here put children at risk. This means that if the problems aren't addressed as early as possible, they will most likely intensify and could have very negative long-term consequences.

Before looking at specific problems, it is important to stress that the lists of signs and symptoms are not all-inclusive, nor will your child exhibit all of the signs and symptoms on them if a problem exists. It is also important to look at these signs and symptoms as part of the big picture. For example, if your adolescent son is doing well in school, is associating with good kids, and hasn't changed in other noticeable ways, don't automatically assume when he shaves his head that he has become involved in a cult. Look at all the variables, including past history. If after doing this you find that your child exhibits a number of the signs or symptoms described over a period of time, you should seek professional help to gain a more accurate assessment of the problem. It is also important to work closely with the school to see if the picture your child presents there matches what you see at home.

Depending on the exact nature of the problem, it is not at all uncommon to see a domino effect: For example, first there is depression, which may lead to substance abuse as a way of trying to deal with the depression, which in turn can result in delinquent behavior when the youngster is under the influence of drugs or alcohol. Although this is not always the pattern, expect that as you begin to peel away the layers to get to the heart of the problem you will find other issues. Some of these issues may indicate changes that need to be made within the family system. Examine the family dynamics and understand that the child or adolescent may be acting out as a way of bringing attention to these underlying family problems.

As you continue reading, remember to consider the frequency, intensity, and duration of the symptoms. In some cases, situational stress has a great impact, and once the situation is resolved, the symptoms disappear. This could be the case with depression. It would be normal to see children or adolescents exhibit depressive symptoms following a divorce in the family or the death of a close friend or relative, but the symptoms should decrease in intensity over time. If this is not the case, intervention is warranted.

A final note: If you find that the behaviors you see or suspect closely match the characteristics described here, don't jump the gun. Although you may be tempted to confront your child or adolescent in an accusatory way, this could make the problem worse by inviting rebellion, especially in adolescents. For example, if you suspect alcohol abuse and accuse your child of it, he or she may respond by getting drunk out of spite. It is also important to proceed cautiously because your child may feel guilty and ashamed or worried about the problem and not want to admit it because to do so would increase his or her feelings of vulnerability or helplessness.

ATTENTION DEFICIT HYPERACTIVITY DISORDER

Attention Deficit Hyperactivity Disorder (ADHD) is probably the most common and complex disorder of children (Goldstein & Goldstein, 1990). This disorder is a combination of problems in children's behavior and thinking that results in inattention, over-arousal, hyperactivity, impulsivity, and demands for immediate gratification.

Bowley and Walther (1992) suggest that from 1 to 10% of American children suffer from ADHD. It is estimated that 3 to 5% of school-age children have this disorder (Paltin, 1993). Boys are diagnosed with ADHD 5 to 10 times more often than girls. However, recent research suggests that as many girls as boys may suffer from ADHD (Hynd, Horn, Voeller, & Marshall, 1991). The symptoms of ADHD in girls are not as obvious as in boys, a factor that may explain why the disorder is less likely to be identified in girls.

For many boys and girls, the onset of ADHD seems to be before age 4, although the disorder may not be formally diagnosed until the child enters school. The disorder persists throughout childhood, with some reduction in hyperactivity occurring in adolescence and adulthood. However, most children diagnosed with ADHD continue to experience trouble concentrating and other difficulties even as adults.

Current thinking reflects the view that the disorder is neuro-biologically based, the result of an imbalance in the brain. A number of factors contribute to ADHD. Heredity is one—ADHD appears to run in families. Another factor is central nervous system abnormalities, such as the presence of neurotoxins, cerebral palsy, or epilepsy. Environmental factors such as an unhappy, stressful, or abusive home setting may also play a part. Diet, especially food additives and sugar, has also been implicated, although its role has recently been questioned.

Parents need to keep in mind that with ADHD the number, severity, and types of symptoms differ from child to child; children display varying degrees of disturbance; and children with ADHD have normal intelligence and show no signs of emotional disturbance.

Signs and Symptoms of Attention Deficit Hyperactivity Disorder

The following signs and symptoms of ADHD as are described by the American Psychiatric Association (1995). The American Psychiatric Association identifies two main types of the disorder: predominantly inattentive and predominantly impulsive-hyperactive. A combined type is also possible.

Inattentive type

With this type, children do not exhibit hyperactive behaviors but have a lot of difficulty concentrating and paying attention. A child is considered to have this type of ADHD if he or she displays at least six of the following symptoms for at least 6 months (American Psychiatric Association, 1995, pp. 83–84).

1. Often fails to give close attention to details or makes careless mistakes in schoolwork, work, or other activities.

2. Often has difficulty sustaining attention in tasks or play activities.

3. Often does not seem to listen to what is being said to him or her.

4. Often does not follow through on instructions and fails to finish schoolwork, chores, or duties in the work place (not due to oppositional behavior or failure to understand instructions).

5. Often has difficulties organizing tasks and activities.

6. Often avoids or strongly dislikes tasks (such as schoolwork or homework) that require sustained mental effort.

7. Often loses things necessary for tasks or activities (e.g., school assignments, pencils, books, tools, or toys).

8. Often forgetful in daily activities.

Hyperactive-impulsive type

The American Psychiatric Association (1995, p. 84) identifies this type in children having at least six of the following symptoms over a period of at least 6 months.

HYPERACTIVITY

1. Often fidgets with hands or feet or squirms in seat.

2. Leaves seat in classroom or in other situations in which remaining seated is expected.

3. Often runs about or climbs excessively in situations where it is inappropriate (in adolescents, may be limited to subjective feelings of restlessness).

4. Often has difficulty playing or engaging in leisure activities quietly.

5. Often talks excessively.

6. Often acts as if "driven by a motor" and cannot remain still.

IMPULSIVITY

7. Often blurts out answers to questions before the questions have been completed.

8. Often has difficulty waiting in lines or awaiting turn in games or group situations.

9. Often interrupts or intrudes on others.

SUICIDE

Suicide has increased dramatically over the past few decades. Although this increase is largely associated with adolescents, there have been more reports in recent years of suicide threats, attempts, and deaths in children under age 10 (Stefanowski-Harding, 1990). It is difficult to find reliable figures for children under age 10 because many of the deaths or attempts are reported as accidents and because parents may attempt to conceal the suicide threat or act because of embarrassment or underestimation of the strength of children's emotions (McGuire & Ely, 1984). It is clear that children under age 10 who threaten or attempt suicide score high on hopelessness scales and that family dynamics such as abuse, violence between parents, ongoing illness of a parent or sibling, or a loss such as a death or divorce are contributing factors (Kazdin, French, Unis, Esveldt-Dawson, & Sherick, 1983). Parents of younger children who are concerned about suicidal tendencies should be aware that sleep disturbance, fatigue, loss of appetite, mood changes, or giving away prized possessions may be indicators that a child is thinking of suicide (Stefanowski-Harding, 1990).

Because adolescent suicide is more prevalent and more is known about it, the focus of the remaining discussion will be on adolescent suicide. Adolescent suicide has increased dramatically over the past few decades. It is considered the second leading cause of death among young people in this country (Cimbolic & Jobes, 1990). Male adolescents are three times more likely to commit suicide than female adolescents, but females are more likely to attempt suicide. This discrepancy may be explained by the fact that males tend to use more lethal methods, such as firearms. Females are more likely to use a less lethal method, such as taking an overdose of pills (Maltsberger, 1988).

According to Santrock (1993), adolescents commit suicide for a variety of reasons. These include stressful circumstances such as family conflict, parental divorce or separation, the death of a parent or friend, the breakup of a romance, a move to a new school, pressure to succeed in school, school failure, or unwanted pregnancy. Other factors involved in suicide may include lack of supportive friendships, depression, confusion about sexual orientation, and substance abuse or eating disorders.

Suicidal adolescents feel they can no longer cope with their problems. Because they still have a relatively immediate sense of time, they cannot see that their problems may get better as time goes on. This is particularly true of adolescents who experience loss of a romantic relationship. They are still so tied to the present and to immediate gratification that they mistakenly assume they will never find another person to love again. As a result, they think suicide is the only way to end the pain.

Parents of adolescents need to be aware of some important myths about suicide, as described by the American Association of Suicidology (1991). First of all, it is a myth to believe that talking to someone about suicidal feelings will cause the person to commit suicide. In fact, talking about suicidal feelings may relieve some of the emotional pain. Another myth is that all suicidal adolescents want to die and that there is nothing that can be done about it. In fact, most suicidal adolescents are ambivalent—that is, they want to die to escape the pain, but they also want to live. It is also a myth to believe that adolescents who talk about committing suicide never actually do it. The fact is that when adolescents talk about suicide, they are giving a warning that should not be ignored. Another myth is that there is a "typical" adolescent who commits suicide. The fact is that the potential for suicide exists in everyone, especially depressed, gifted, or gay and lesbian adolescents. There is no such thing as the "typical" suicidal person. Finally, it is a myth to believe that suicide occurs without warning. The fact is that many adolescents do give warning of their suicidal intent in the form of notes, comments, or behaviors.

Signs and Symptoms of Adolescent Suicide Risk

The following warning signs of suicide risk in adolescents have been derived from Richman (1986) and Herring (1990).

1. Withdrawal from family members and friends. This is often not recognized because adolescents normally withdraw from family and may go through periods of withdrawal from friends.

2. Dramatic changes in the suicidal person's behavior. For example, an outgoing, cheerful adolescent may become withdrawn and uncommunicative, displaying feelings of sadness. Or an adolescent who has typically been quiet may begin acting out and getting into trouble.

3. Experiencing increased failure at school, home, and work, as well as in friendships and love relationships. This symptom is manifested most clearly in school performance.

4. Recent family changes, such as illness, parental job loss, increased drinking by parents or other family members, or relocation. Other triggers may be loss of a family member through death, divorce, separation, or leaving home.

5. Feelings of despair and hopelessness. These feelings may be manifested in many forms, including changes in posture or dress, as well as behavioral and verbal expressions.

6. Symptomatic acts, such as a series of accidents or impulsive risk-taking behaviors, drug or alcohol abuse, inappropriate aggressiveness or submissiveness, or giving away prized possessions

7. Communication of suicidal thoughts or feelings in statements such as "Life is not worth living," "I'm finished," "I'm done for," "I might as well be dead," or "I wish I were dead"

8. Presence of a plan, such as storing up medication or buying a gun

9. A prior suicide attempt. It is estimated that four out of five people who commit suicide have made at least one previous attempt.

10. Preoccupation with death, which the adolescent may display in music, art, and personal writing

11. Disturbances in the adolescent's sleeping, eating, and personal hygiene habits

12. The recent suicide of a classmate or friend

DEPRESSION

Depression affects many adolescents and is becoming more common among younger children (Rutter, 1986). It is often difficult to detect childhood depression because younger children have a hard time verbalizing their feelings and may express their depression through a variety of behaviors. It is also difficult to pinpoint adolescent depression because of the fine distinction between the normal mood swings characteristic of this period and more serious depression.

Sometimes childhood depression is manifested by sadness, feelings of discouragement and helplessness, and low self-esteem. However, it is also very typical to see young children communicate their depression through poor school performance, refusal to attend school, boredom, or problems with friends. Family problems such as divorce, violence, alcoholism, or abuse are some of the factors that can precipitate childhood depression (Hart, 1991).

There are several possible causes of depression during adolescence (Parrott, 1993). First, biochemical factors such as changes in hormone levels can contribute to feelings of depression. Changes in hormone levels may be the result of some medications, improper diet, or lack of sleep. A second cause relates to the adolescent's life experiences—for example, inability to meet one's own or parental expectations, to fit in with a peer group, or to succeed in school, sports, or other activities. A third cause of depression involves the responses others make. Although any depression is serious and warrants concern, excessive attention and sympathy may actually reinforce the depressed symptoms. Learned helplessness, or the sense that nothing can be done to change the situation, is a fourth cause of depression. In this case, the adolescent gives up trying, which further compounds his or her feelings of depression. The fifth cause of depression is negative thinking. The adolescent with a negative view of self and the world can trigger a downward spiral of depression: The feeling of worthlessness and the belief that there is no future causes the youngster to feel depressed. As a result of the depression, the adolescent does not reach out to others for support nor attempt to succeed in school. In turn, he or she is lonely and fails in school, which reinforces the notion of worthlessness and incompetence. Finally, any type of loss is a major factor in adolescent depression (Berk, 1993). This could include the loss of friends or family through death; loss associated with a change in significant relationships; loss associated with divorce, abuse, or neglect; or the loss of the routine and familiarity of high school after graduation.

Signs and Symptoms of Adolescent Depression

Because adolescent depression is more common than childhood depression, we include here a list of specific signs and symptoms pertaining to adolescent depression (American Psychiatric Association, 1995, p. 327). At least five of the symptoms must have been present over a 2-week period. These symptoms must represent a change from previous behavior.

1. Depressed mood (irritable mood) most of the day, nearly every day, as indicated either by subjective account or observation by others

2. Markedly diminished interest or pleasure in all, or almost all, activities most of the day, nearly every

day (as indicated either by subjective account or observation by others of apathy most of the time)

3. Significant weight loss or weight gain when not dieting (e.g., more than 5% of body weight in a month), or decrease or increase in appetite nearly every day

4. Insomnia or hypersomnia nearly every day

5. Psychomotor agitation or slowing down nearly every day (observed by others, not merely subjective feelings of restlessness or being slowed down)

6. Fatigue or loss of energy nearly every day

7. Feelings of worthlessness or excessive or inappropriate guilt (which may be delusional) nearly every day (not merely self-reproach or guilt about being sick)

8. Diminished ability to think or concentrate, or indecisiveness, nearly every day (either by subjective account or as observed by others)

9. Recurrent thoughts of death (not just fear of dying), recurrent suicidal ideation without a specific plan, or a suicide attempt or a specific plan for committing suicide

DELINQUENT BEHAVIOR

Delinquency in its legal sense refers to the behavior of children under age 18 who commit illegal acts such as stealing, forgery, breaking and entering, or mugging. Such children may also run away from home, be truant from school, or engage in other socially unacceptable behaviors.

A number of factors predispose children or adolescents to delinquency. According to Santrock (1993), delinquents have not developed sufficient behavioral self-control to prevent them from committing illegal acts. A contributing problem is the difficulty they have in delaying gratification. They think they should have immediate satisfaction and shouldn't have to work for what they want. This pattern contributes to cheating and stealing.

The family also plays a major role in fostering or deterring delinquent behavior. Parents who rarely monitor their children's activities, provide little support, and ineffectively discipline may be encouraging delinquent behavior. Peers can also contribute to delinquency. Children who have strongly influential delinquent friends are more likely to become delinquent themselves.

Signs and Symptoms of Delinquent Behavior

Many delinquent behaviors are included in the diagnosis of conduct disorder. The American Psychiatric Association (1995, p. 90) identifies the following signs and symptoms as indicating the presence of this disorder. At least three of the signs must have been exhibited in the past 12 months, with at least one behavior having been present for at least 6 months. The signs and symptoms are grouped under four general categories: aggression to people and animals, destruction of property, deceitfulness or theft, and serious violations of rules.

Aggression to people and animals

1. Often bullies, threatens, or intimidates others.

2. Often initiates physical fights.

3. Has used a weapon that can cause serious physical harm to others (for example, a bat, brick, broken bottle, knife, gun).

4. Has been physically cruel to people.

5. Has been physically cruel to animals.

6. Has stolen while confronting a victim (for example, mugging, purse snatching, extortion, armed robbery).

7. Has forced someone into sexual activity.

Destruction of property

8. Has deliberately engaged in fire setting with the intention of causing serious damage.

9. Has deliberately destroyed others' property (other than by fire setting).

Deceitfulness or theft

10. Has broken into someone else's house, building, or car.

11. Often lies to obtain goods or favors or to avoid obligations (in other words, "cons" others).

12. Has stolen items of nontrivial value without confronting a victim (for example, shoplifting, but without breaking and entering; forgery).

Serious violations of rules

13. Often stays out at night despite parental prohibitions, beginning before age 13.

14. Has run away from home overnight at least twice while living in parental or parental surrogate home (or once without returning for a lengthy period).

15. Is often truant from school, beginning before age 13.

EATING DISORDERS

Young people are growing up in a culture that focuses excessively on appearance. Stereotypes of the perfect body image exert a great deal of pressure on children, especially adolescents, to conform to ideal standards of beauty. In their efforts to conform, an increasing number of adolescents, especially females, are at risk for developing eating disorders.

The two most serious eating disorders are anorexia and bulimia. With anorexia, young people starve themselves because of an intense fear of becoming obese. Anorexics have an extremely distorted body image, believing they are still fat even after becoming severely underweight. They often come from high-achieving families who place a lot of importance on academic performance. Anorexics exercise excessively and are obsessed with food. They may like to prepare food for others as a way of controlling what is served, but they eat only a minimal amount themselves. The majority of anorexics are female.

Anorexics lose 25 to 50% of their body weight and appear extremely thin (Akeroyd-Guillory, 1988). The severe loss of weight interferes with the female's menstrual cycle. Anorexics' skin becomes pale and extremely dry; their nails are discolored and brittle; their hair thins, dries, and becomes dull; fine hair appears all over the body; and they become sensitive to cold because they have no protective fat layer. Other physical complications include electrolyte imbalance, cardiac distress, susceptibility to disease, and severe fatigue. Continued weight loss can result in heart shrinkage, kidney failure, and death (Harris, 1991).

The second type of eating disorder, bulimia, is more prevalent in females but is also seen in adolescent males, especially wrestlers. Bulimia differs from anorexia in that bulimics eat large amounts of food at one time (binging), followed by self-induced vomiting, heavy doses of laxatives, or strict dieting (purging). Bulimia is much more common than anorexia (Edelstein, Haskew, & Kramer, 1989).

Like anorexics, bulimics are afraid of getting fat, often come from affluent families with high expectations, and have distorted body images. Unlike anorexics, bulimics tend to be impulsive eaters, may abuse alcohol, and may steal to get money to support their binges. Bulimics may be more aware of their abnormal eating patterns than anorexics, partly because they have to work harder to hide their binging and purging behavior. Because of these more noticeable behaviors, bulimia is easier to detect. It is also generally easier to treat than anorexia (Harris, 1991). Bulimics are, as a rule, more aware than anorexics that their eating behavior is out of control.

Signs and Symptoms of Anorexia

The following signs and symptoms of anorexia are reported by Akeroyd-Guillory (1988).

1. Extreme weight loss (25 to 50% of body weight)

2. Extreme dissatisfaction with and distortion of body image

3. Excessive exercise through jogging, walking, swimming, or working out to burn off calories

4. Intense worry about food—when to eat, how much to eat, and what to eat. Food intake is very controlled. Anorexics usually have a mental list of "safe" foods, which generally includes no meat, restricted amounts of dairy products, and no sweets. Specific "safe foods" vary with the individual.

5. In females, discontinuation of the menstrual cycle

6. Excessive guilt if they eat more than they think they should and do not exercise it off

7. Frequent weighing of self, sometimes every hour

8. Withdrawal from social situations, especially occasions that include food

9. Frequent mood swings, irritability, defiance, stubbornness, intolerance of change, and low self-esteem

Signs and Symptoms of Bulimia

The following signs and symptoms of bulimia are reported by Omizo and Omizo (1992).

1. Rapid weight gain and weight loss

2. Secretive binges in which large amounts of food are consumed, followed by vomiting

3. Noticeable physical abnormalities—scars on the fingers that have been used to induce vomiting, erosion of tooth enamel due to effects of stomach acids, and swollen glands (which look like the mumps) from vomiting

4. Extreme dissatisfaction with and distortion of body image

5. Frequent bathroom trips, indicating possible vomiting or laxative abuse, and frequent weighing of self, especially before and after a binge

6. Feelings of depression, irritability, anger, guilt, apathy, or loneliness

7. Low self-esteem

DRUG AND ALCOHOL ABUSE

Many adolescents experiment with cigarettes, alcohol, marijuana, cocaine, and other drugs. Some use them out of curiosity, while others use them to reduce tension, frustration, boredom, or fatigue. Many use drugs to fit in with peers and, in some cases, to escape reality. While they may derive temporary feelings of inner peace, joy, relaxation, surges of exhilaration, or prolonged heightened sensation, the long-range effects of drug use, including the use of alcohol, are serious—drug dependence and susceptibility to serious and even fatal diseases.

Alcohol is the drug of choice for most adolescents. Since alcohol impairs motor performance, depth perception, reaction time, and night vision, an adolescent under the influence of alcohol presents a considerable risk to self and others when driving. Automobile accidents are the leading cause of death among adolescents, and alcohol is implicated in many of these accidents (Balk, 1994). Alcohol abuse also has some serious long-term effects, including damage to the heart, the central nervous system, and the liver. It increases risk for high blood pressure and destroys brain cells.

Many parents are relieved if their adolescent is using alcohol as opposed to other drugs. They tend to overlook the seriousness of alcohol as a problem because of misconceptions or myths. One myth is "It's only beer." However, since the key ingredient in all alcoholic beverages is alcohol, beer has the same potential as other alcoholic beverages to cause intoxication and lead to addiction. Another myth is reflected in the common remark "What harm can a few drinks do?" The fact is that alcohol first affects the area in the brain that controls judgment and self-control. That is why people under the influence of alcohol may say or do things they later regret. Another myth is related to the idea that since many adults drink without having problems, why can't teens? The answer is that it is illegal for teens in most countries to buy or consume alcohol. More important, adolescent alcohol consumption can have significant negative effects on growth and development. Associated with this myth is the belief that teenagers can't become alcoholics. In fact, alcoholism in younger people develops more rapidly, sometimes within 6 months after the first drink. An additional myth is that "It can't happen to my child." It can and does.

Signs and Symptoms of Alcohol Abuse

Some of the signs and symptoms of alcohol abuse are as follows (Parrott, 1993).

1. Slurred speech or lack of coordination, staggering

2. Use of gum, mint, or mouthwash to mask alcohol on the breath

3. Excessive sleeping, especially at unusual times

4. Deterioration in school performance, reflected by inconsistent or poor grades, increased absenteeism, or tardiness

5. Physical complaints about feeling sick or actual sickness (especially headaches or nausea)

6. Frequent, abrupt mood swings

7. Social withdrawal—isolation from family, friends, or social activities

8. Increased social activities, which often includes a change in friendships

9. Dishonesty

Signs and Symptoms of Drug Abuse

Signs and symptoms of drug abuse include the following (Steinberg & Levine, 1990).

1. Possession of drug paraphernalia, such as pipes, rolling papers, or other drug items

2. Odor of drugs or use of cover-ups (incense, sprays)

3. Identification with the drug culture, as shown by drug-related magazines or slogans on clothing

4. Signs of physical deterioration, such as memory lapses, short attention span, difficulty concentrating, unhealthy appearance, bloodshot eyes, dilated pupils, and changes in activity levels (lethargic or hyperactive)

5. Dramatic changes in school performance, reflected in lower grades and increased absenteeism or tardiness

6. Changes in behavior, such as chronic dishonesty; changes in friends; possession of large sums of money; increasing, inappropriate anger; mood swings; reduced motivation, self-discipline, and self-esteem; and indifference to grooming

SEXUAL ABUSE

Sexual abuse of children and adolescents is no longer a rare occurrence. Recent statistics indicate that 1 of every 4 girls and 1 of every 7 to 10 boys will have been sexually abused by the age of 18 (Hackbarth, Murphy, & McQuary, 1991). This does not reflect the actual occurrence. Many children and adolescents are reluctant to tell because they feel frightened, confused, and guilty. In addition, they are usually pressured by their abusers to keep the secret.

Sexual abuse ranges from sexual comments and fondling to intercourse and even sodomy. Although most sexual abuse occurs during middle childhood, it can occur at all ages. Few children or adolescents experience only one episode of sexual abuse, and for some the abuse continues for many years (Gomez-Schwartz, Horowitz, & Cardarelli, 1990). The perpetrator is generally male and is most likely to be known to the child—a parent, relative, baby-sitter, or someone else who comes in contact with the child on a regular basis and whom the child knows well and trusts.

According to Faller (1990), consequences of sexual abuse include a child's tendency to frequently display sexual knowledge and behavior beyond what is appropriate for his or her age, to believe that sexual overtures are an acceptable way to get attention, and to become promiscuous and involved in unhealthy relationships as a young adult. When children who have been abused become parents, they often have poor parenting skills and abuse and neglect their own children, thus transmitting the abuse to the next generation.

Signs and Symptoms of Sexual Abuse

Specific signs and symptoms of sexual abuse are as follows. These have been derived from Berk (1994), the Parental Stress Center (1982), and Tennant (1988).

1. For preschoolers: Regression, as demonstrated by thumb sucking, clinging behavior, fear of being with certain people they were once comfortable with, bed wetting, fear of the dark, being afraid to sleep alone, and overeating or undereating

2. For school-age children: Development of physical symptoms, such as sore throat and stomach pains; disturbed concentration; undereating; and discomfort about being with certain people. They may also be afraid to sleep alone or may wet the bed.

3. For adolescents: Depression, low self-esteem, fear of being touched, mistrust of adults, anger and hostility, difficulties in getting along with peers, drug and alcohol abuse, suicide attempts, refusal to participate in gym classes, running away from home, and promiscuous behavior

4. For children of all ages, the following types of physical symptoms: Vaginal discharge; unexplained pain, itching,

or discomfort in the genital area; difficulty walking or sitting; and venereal disease. Also note changes in school behavior, such as disruptive behavior, decline in academic performance, and increased absenteeism. Drawings or paintings with dominant sexual themes are also an important indicator.

CULT INVOLVEMENT

Although we'd like to think that adolescents are immune to cult involvement, in reality there are more than 2,500 cults in the United States (Santrock, 1993). Cult leaders use various means to gain control over members' minds. Once under the control of the cult, members may be instructed to memorize chants, experiment with drugs, and told to associate with and marry only other cult members (Galanter, 1989).

Some adolescents are particularly susceptible to cults because they are disillusioned with organized religion, are experiencing family disruption, and want to be a part of a group. In addition, they may be idealistic and have a strong desire to help others, improve society, and know God better. Cult recruiters manipulate this idealism by convincing adolescents that they can achieve these goals only within the particular group. Innocence is another adolescent characteristic that makes young people susceptible to the lure of cults—specifically, adolescents may believe that everyone who speaks in the name of God is sincere and trustworthy. Inquisitive adolescents can fall prey to the call of cults because they seek groups to join to discuss various issues and find answers to questions. Adolescents who have become independent of their parents for the first time are targeted by cult recruiters who realize that these teens might be lonely and are more susceptible to invitations for free meals and fellowship. Finally, identity-seeking adolescents are vulnerable to cults because as they clarify their identities, they begin to question value systems, goals, and religion.

Signs and Symptoms of Cult Involvement

The following are signs and symptoms that might be seen in youth who are involved in cults (Burket, Myers, Lyles, & Carrera, 1994; Warnke Ministries, 1986; Young, 1990).

1. The presence of books about cults or satanism

CHAPTER 7

2. Possession of cult-related paraphernalia, jewelry, or clothing, including shrines, candles, incense, or black robes

3. Changes in behavior and appearance, such as shaving the head to conform to a cult's teachings or rituals or engaging in self-mutilation by cutting the left side of the arm, ankle, or chest

4. Use of certain symbols, such as the upside-down cross or backward swastika in a circle with a lightning bolt

5. Cruelty to animals, in cases where animal sacrifices are part of the cult's rituals

6. Depression, aggressiveness, sleep disorders, anger, anxiety, suicide attempts, or substance abuse

7. Daily listening to heavy metal music with violent lyrics

CONCLUSION

As parents, we all hope our children and adolescents won't have to experience any of the problems described in this chapter. However, some will. Not only are these problems of a serious nature, but many can encourage a multitude of other equally serious problems—early sexual activity, teen pregnancy, sexually transmitted diseases, school dropout, or violent activity. It's not a pretty picture.

We have not included suggestions for dealing with the problems described here because we firmly believe that professional help is a must. Professionals who are trained to help children, adolescents, and families with problems such as these can intervene and assist. Remember that problems that exist today don't have to affect your child or your family forever: These problems can be treated.

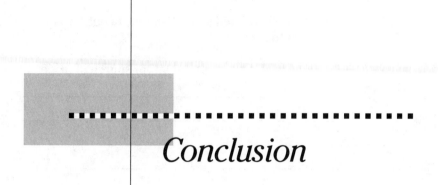

Conclusion

A wise parent recently said, "Parenting is a job you can never resign, retire, or be fired from." Those of you who are still worrying about your 20-year-old probably agree with this! And although there are days, weeks, or even months when we might like to resign or retire, these times pass for most parents; some even wish they could live it all over again!

As we conclude this book, we invite you to reflect on your parenting process. Take a few minutes to complete the following short activity, which we hope will help you put in perspective what you've been reading about.

First, identify your child/children by name and age. Then think of one word that best describes your child/children.

Child's name	Age	Descriptive word
_____	_____	_____
_____	_____	_____
_____	_____	_____
_____	_____	_____

Next think about each child's greatest gift, talent, or source of pride for you. List these.

Child's name	Gift, talent, or source of pride
_____	_____
_____	_____
_____	_____
_____	_____
_____	_____

Now think about the greatest nonmaterial gift or hope for the future you'd like to share with each child. List.

Child's name	Gift to your child
_____	_____
_____	_____
_____	_____
_____	_____
_____	_____

And last, think about your strengths as a parent; what are you most proud of? It's time to give yourself a pat on the back for tackling the most important job of your life.

Your strengths

_____

_____

_____

_____

In conclusion, we'd like to share the following adaptation of a poem by Dorothy Law Nolte, which we feel summarizes many of the points stressed in this book:

If children live with criticism,
they learn to condemn.

If children live with hostility,
they learn to fight.

If children live with ridicule,
they learn to be shy.

If children live with shame,
they learn to feel guilty.

If children live with tolerance,
they learn to be patient.

If children live with encouragement,
they learn confidence.

If children live with praise,
they learn to appreciate.

If children live with fairness,
they learn justice.

If children live with security,
they learn to have faith.

If children live with approval,
they learn to like themselves.

If children live with acceptance and friendship,
they learn to find love in the world.

References

Akeroyd-Guillory, D. (1988). A developmental view of anorexia nervosa. *The School Counselor, 36*(1), 24–33.

American Association of Suicidology. (1991). *Suicide: Myths and facts.* Denver, CO: Author.

American Psychiatric Association. (1995). *Diagnostic and statistical manual of mental disorders* (4th ed.). Washington, DC: Author.

Balk, D. E. (1994). *Adolescent development: Early through late adolescence.* Pacific Grove, CA: Brooks/Cole.

Barrish, I. J., & Barrish, H. H. (1986). *Surviving and enjoying your adolescent.* Kansas City, MO: Westport.

Berk, L. E. (1994). *Child development* (3rd ed.). New York: Allyn & Bacon.

Bernard, M. (1984). *Rational emotive therapy with children and adolescents.* New York: Wiley.

Bowley, B. A., & Walther, E. (1992). Attention deficit disorders and the role of the elementary school counselor. *Elementary School Guidance and Counseling, 27*(1), 39–46.

Burket, R. C., Myers, W. C., Lyles, W. B., & Carrera, F. (1994). Emotional and behavioral disturbances in adolescents involved in witchcraft and satanism. *Journal of Adolescence, 17,* 41–52.

171

Butterfield, S. A., & Loovis, M. (1993). Influence of age, sex, balance and sport participation on development of throwing by children in grades K–8. *Perceptual and Motor Skills, 76,* 459–464.

Carroll, L. (1971). *Alice in wonderland.* New York: W. W. Norton.

Cimbolic, P., & Jobes, D. A. (1990). *Youth suicide: Issues, assessment, and intervention.* Springfield, IL: Charles C Thomas.

Coopersmith, S. (1967). *The antecedents of self-esteem.* San Francisco: W. H. Freeman.

Cratty, B. (1974). *Psychomotor behavior in education and sport.* Springfield, IL: Charles C Thomas.

Dinkmeyer, D., & Losoncy, L. E. (1980). *The encouragement book.* Englewood Cliffs, NJ: Prentice-Hall.

Dreikurs, R., & Grey, L. (1968). *Logical consequences: A handbook of discipline.* New York: Meredith.

Dreikurs, R., & Soltz, V. (1964). *Children: The challenge.* New York: Duell, Sloan and Pearce.

Edelstein, C. K., Haskew, P., & Kramer, J. P. (1989, August 15). Early clues to anorexia and bulimia. *Patient Care,* pp. 155–175.

Eisenberg, N. (1987). The relation of altruism and other moral behaviors to moral cognition: Methodological and conceptual issues. In N. Eisenberg (Ed.), *Contemporary topics in developmental psychology.* New York: Wiley.

Elkind, D. (1984). *All grown up and no place to go: Teenagers in crisis.* Reading, MA: Addison-Wesley.

Elkind, D. (1988). *The hurried child: Growing up too fast too soon.* Reading, MA: Addison-Wesley.

Ellis, A., Moseley, S., & Wolfe, J. (1966). *How to raise an emotionally healthy, happy child.* Hollywood, CA: Wilshire.

Faller, K. C. (1990). *Understanding child sexual maltreatment.* Newbury Park, CA: Sage.

Frank, A. (1963). *Anne Frank: The diary of a young girl.* New York: Washington Square.

Freud, S. (1974). *The Freud/Jung letters: The correspondence between Sigmund Freud and C. G. Yung.* Princeton, NJ: Princeton University Press.

Galanter, M. (1989). *Cults: Faith, healing, and coercion.* New York: Oxford University Press.

Galinsky, E. (1981). *Between generations: The six stages of parenthood.* New York: Times Books.

Goldstein, S., & Goldstein, M. (1990). *Managing attention disorders in children: A guide for practitioners.* New York: Wiley.

Gomez-Schwartz, B., Horowitz, J. M., & Cardarelli, A. P. (1990). *Child sexual abuse: Initial effects.* Newbury Park, CA: Sage.

Gordon, T. (1970). *Parent Effectiveness Training: The tested way to raise responsible children.* New York: Peter H. Wyden.

Gordon, T. (1975). *P.E.T.: Parent Effectiveness Training.* New York: New American Library.

Hackbarth, S. G., Murphy, H. D., & McQuary, J. P. (1991). Identifying sexually abused children by using kinetic family drawings. *Elementary School Guidance and Counseling, 25*(4), 255–260.

Harris, P. L. (1991). Anorexia nervosa and bulimia nervosa in female adolescents. *Nutrition Today, 26*(2), 30–34.

Hart, S. L. (1991). Childhood depression: Implications and options for school counselors. *Elementary School Guidance and Counseling, 25*(4), 277–289.

Havighurst, R. J. (1972). *Developmental tasks and education.* New York: David McKay.

Herring, R. (1990). Suicide in the middle school: Who said kids will not? *Elementary School Guidance and Counseling, 25*(2), 129–137.

Hoffman, M. (1970). Moral development. In P. H. Mussen (Ed.), *Carmichael's manual of child psychology.* New York: Wiley.

Hohenshil, T. H., & Brown, M. B. (1991). Public school counseling services for prekindergarten children. *Elementary School Guidance and Counseling, 26*(1), 4–11.

Howe, J. (1986). *There is a monster under my bed.* New York: Atheneum.

Hynd, G. W., Horn, K. L., Voeller, K. K., & Marshall, R. M. (1991). Neurobiological basis of attention-deficit hyperactivity disorder (ADHD). *School Psychology Review, 20*, 174–186.

Kazdin, A. E., French, N. H., Unis, A. S., Esveldt-Dawson, K., & Sherick, R. B. (1983). Hopelessness, depression, and suicidal intent among psychiatrically disturbed inpatient children. *Journal of Consulting and Clinical Psychology, 51*, 504–510.

Main, F. (1986). *Perfect parenting and other myths.* Minneapolis: Comprehensive Care Corporation.

Maltsberger, J. T. (1988). *Suicide risk.* New York: Human Services Press.

Meyerhoff, M. K., & White, B. L. (1986, September). Making the grade as parents. *Psychology Today*, pp. 38–45.

Martin, B., Jr. (1987). *Knots on a counting rope.* New York: Holt.

McGuire, D., & Ely, M. (1984). Child suicide. *Child Welfare, 1*, 17–26.

Nelsen, J., & Lott, L. (1991). *I'm on your side.* Rocklin, CA: Prima.

Omizo, S. A., & Omizo, M. M. (1992). Eating disorders: The school counselor's role. *The School Counselor, 39*(3), 217–224.

Paltin, D. M. (1993). *The parents' hyperactivity handbook: Helping the fidgety child.* New York: Plenum.

Parental Stress Center. (1982). *Early identification of sexual abuse.* Madison, WI: Author.

Parrott, L. (1993). *Helping the struggling adolescent.* Grand Rapids, MI: Zondervan.

Phelan, T. W. (1993). *Surviving your adolescents.* Glen Ellyn, IL: Child Management.

Piaget, J. (1950). *The psychology of intelligence.* New York: International Universities Press.

Piper, W. (1961). *The little engine that could.* New York: Platt & Munk.

Powell, R. (1990). *How to deal with monsters.* Mahwah, NJ: Troll.

Richman, J. (1986). *Family therapy for suicidal people.* New York: Springer.

Rutter, M. L. (1986). Child psychiatry: The interface between clinical and developmental research. *Psychological Medicine, 16,* 151–169.

Santrock, J. W. (1993). *Adolescence: An introduction.* Dubuque, IA: William C. Brown.

Schave, D., & Schave, B. (1989). *Early adolescence and the search for self.* New York: Praeger.

Seifert, K. L., & Hoffnung, R. J. (1993). *Child and adolescent development* (2nd ed). Boston: Houghton Mifflin.

Stefanowski-Harding, S. (1990). Child suicide: A review of the literature and implications for school counselors. *Elementary School Guidance and Counseling, 37*(5), 328–336.

Steinberg, L. D., & Levine, A. (1987). *You and your adolescent.* New York: Harper Perennial.

Steinberg, L. D., & Levine, A. (1990). *You and your adolescent: A parent's guide for ages 10 to 20.* New York: Harper & Row.

Tennant, C. G. (1988). Preventive sexual abuse programs: Problems and possibilities. *Elementary School Guidance and Counseling, 23,* 48–53.

Vernon, A. (1993). *Developmental assessment and intervention with children and adolescents.* Alexandria, VA: American Counseling Association.

Warnke Ministries. (1986). *The philosophy and practice of satanism: A preliminary study of satanism and occult-related crime.* Danville, KY: Author.

Young, J. (1990, February 22). Watch kids for satanic "dabbling." *Lincoln Journal Star.*

Index

Abuse, 22, 40
 and ADHD, 151
 and depression, 117–118, 155, 156
 and suicidal tendencies, 153
 See also specific kinds
Achievement, sense of,
 in middle childhood, 86–87, 88
 in preschool years, 54–55, 56, 67
ADHD (Attention Deficit Hyperactivity
  Disorder), 150–152
Admonishing (communication roadblock), 28
Adolescence,
 cult involvement in, 149, 165–166
 delinquent behavior in, 157–159
 depression in, 155–157
 discipline guide for parents on, 41,
  48, 49–51
 eating disorders in, 159–161
 and "I" messages, 33–35
 and interpretive stage of
  parenting, 23–24
 and permissive parents, 17–18
 problem solving in, 46–47
 sexual abuse in, 163–165
 substance abuse in, 161–163
 suicides in, 153–155

See also Early adolescence;
  Mid-adolescence
Advising (communication roadblock),
  29, 35
Aggression. *See* Delinquent behavior
Agreeing (communication roadblock), 30
AIDS, 5, 102, 127, 128–129
Akeroyd-Guillory, D., 159, 160
Alcohol abuse. *See* Substance abuse
Alice in Wonderland (Carroll), 132
American Association of Suicidology,
  153–154
American Psychiatric Association,
  151–152, 156, 158
Analyzing (communication roadblock), 31
Anger of children,
 and bulimia, 161
 and cult involvement, 166
 in early adolescence, 116–118, 139
 and leaving home, 139
 in tantrums, 72, 73–74
Anger of parent,
 from irrational beliefs, 6–11
 in parenting styles and stages, 16,
  18, 22
 over serious problems, 146
 over willful behavior, 68

175

About the Authors

Ann Vernon, PhD, NCC, LMHC, is professor and coordinator of the counselor education program, Department of Educational Administration and Counseling, University of Northern Iowa, Cedar Falls. In addition, Dr. Vernon maintains a part-time private practice where she specializes in working with children, adolescents, and their parents. In addition to teaching and counseling, Dr. Vernon is a frequent speaker at professional conferences and conducts workshops throughout the United States and Canada on a variety of topics pertaining to children and adolescents. She is the author of the *Thinking, Feeling, Behaving* (Research Press, 1989) emotional education curricula for children and adolescents, *Developmental Assessment and Intervention with Children and Adolescents* (American Counseling Association, 1993), and numerous chapters in books on rational-emotive therapy with children and adolescents, creative counseling techniques, and emotional education. She is also the director of the Midwest Center for Rational-Emotive Therapy.

Radhi Al-Mabuk, PhD, is an assistant professor of education in the Department of Educational Psychology, University of Northern Iowa, Cedar Falls. Dr. Al-Mabuk is a native of Awamiyah, Saudi Arabia, and has been living in the United States since 1976.

He received his bachelor's degree in social studies education from St. Mary's College, Winona, Minnesota; his master's degree in counseling from Winona State University; and his doctorate in educational psychology with emphasis on human development from the University of Wisconsin at Madison. In addition to teaching courses on human development from infancy through adolescence, Dr. Al-Mabuk conducts research and workshops on the psychology of forgiveness, especially its use as a conflict resolution strategy in the context of deep parent-child conflict. He has published a number of articles on the topic and is now writing a book about the psychological process of forgiveness.